Sinbad the Sailor

A Pantomime

John Crocker

A SAMUEL FRENCH ACTING EDITION

SAMUEL FRENCH

FOUNDED 1830

SAMUELFRENCH-LONDON.CO.UK
SAMUELFRENCH.COM

FOR AMATEUR PRODUCTION ENQUIRIES

UNITED KINGDOM AND WORLD EXCLUDING NORTH AMERICA

plays@SamuelFrench-London.co.uk

020 7255 4302/01

Each title is subject to availability from Samuel French,

depending upon country of performance.

CHARACTERS

SINBAD
MRS SINBAD .... his mother
DRUSILA .... a dromedary
CALIPH OF BAGHDAD*
PRINCESS YASMIN .... his daughter
TINBAD .... the tailor
The PERI
The OLD MAN OF THE SEA
ALI WHEY
BAK ALI .... two nautical ne'er do wells
BLACKBEARD* .... a giant
SLAVE MASTER*
VIZIER* .... to the KHEDIVE
KHEDIVE OF EGYPT*
KING SERENDIB* .... an Indian King

*These parts can be doubled.

CHORUS as TOWNSFOLK, STREET TRADERS, CALIPH'S GUARDS,
        SAILORS, PIRATES, DIAMONDS, SLAVES, KHEDIVE'S
        ATTENDANTS, KING SERENDIB'S WIVES ETC.

CHILDREN as STREET URCHINS, PIGMIES, MONKEYS, CENTIPEDE,
        KHEDIVE S ATTENDANTS and one CHILD as LITTLE
        OLD MAN OF THE SEA.
++

PRODUCTION NOTE

Pantomime, as we know it today, is a form of entertainment all on its own, derived from a number of different sources - the commedia dell'arte (and all that that derived from), the ballet, opera, music hall and the realms of folklore and fairy tale - and elements of all these are still to be found in it. This strange mixture has created a splendid topsy-turvy world where men are women, women are men, where the present is embraced within the past, where people are hit but not hurt, where authority is constantly flouted, where everything is open to ridicule - including pantomime itself at times - and where, above all, magic abounds and dreams invariably come true. In other words, it is - or should be - fun. Fun to do and fun to watch and the sense of enjoyment which can be conveyed by a cast is very important to the enjoyment of an audience.

Pantomime can be very simply staged if resources are limited. Basically a tab surround at the back, tab legs at the sides and a set of traverse tabs for the frontcloth scenes, together with the simplest of cut-out pieces to suggest various locales — or even just placards with this information written on them — will suffice. Conversely, there is no limit to the extent to which more lavish facilities can be employed and, if they are available, SINBAD THE SAILOR offers wide scope for spectacular effects.

The directions I have given in the text adopt a middle course and are based on a permanent setting of a cyclorama sky-cloth at the back, a few feet in front of which is a rostrum about two feet high running the width of the stage. About two-thirds of the depth DS is a false proscenium, immediately behind which are the lines for a set of traverse tabs. Below the false proscenium are arched entrances L and R, with reveals if necessary to the proscenium. A border will be required at some point between the false proscenium and the cyclorama to mask the lighting battens and the top of the cyclorama. Lastly, there are sets of steps leading down into the auditorium at both front corners of the stage.

Into this permanent setting are placed cut-out backings and various wings L and R. The frontcloth fly lines come in behind the traverse tabs. Cloths can , of course, be tumbled or rolled if flying space is limited. I have indicated that the traverse tabs should be closed for the beginning of most frontcloth scenes then,if any hitch occurs while flying in the cloth,the lights can come up and the actors get on with the scene. Similarly I have, where possible, given cues before the ends of these scenes for the tabs to be closed again to allow time for the cloths to be flown out. Thus, each scene can flow swiftly into the next, an important point if a smooth-running production is to be achieved.

The settings and costumes should preferably be in clear, bright colours to give a story-bock effect. Obviously the costumes must be eastern in style, but deliberate incongruities can be introduced into some of the comics' costumes. Animal skins can be hired from Theatre Zoo, 28 New Row, London, WC2N 4LA. 01-836 3150.

The Strobe Freeze Light and the Cloud Lantern can be hired from the usual stage electrical suppliers; the maroons and the flash boxes and powder used throughout can also be obtained from them. I have not attempted to give a complete lighting plot as this depends entirely on the equipment available but, generally speaking, most pantomime lighting needs to be full-up, warm and bright. Pinks and ambers are probably best for this and a circuit of blues in the cyclorama battens would be useful for the evening lighting and any other dramatic effects. Follow spots are a great help but not essential. If they are used it is often effective in romantic numbers to fade out the stage lighting and hold the principals in the follow spots and then quickly fade up to the full lighting on the last few bars as this can help to increase applause!

Pantomime needs many props and often they will have to be homemade. Instructions are given in SPECIAL INSTRUCTIONS for any of the more complicated ones. They should be colourfully painted and, in pantomime, many of them should be larger then in real life. It is also wise for the property master to examine carefully the practical use to which any prop is to be put; a whole comedy sequence can be ruined because something does not work properly, and one of the cast can be 'ruined' if he has to be hit with a club made of solid wood instead of material filled with foam rubber!

The music has been specially composed so that it is easy for the less musically accomplished to master, but it is also scored in parts for the more ambitious. If an orchestra is available well and good, but a single piano will suffice. It is an advantage, however, to have a drummer as well; not only because a rhythmic accompaniment enhances the numbers but because, for some reason never fully fathomed, slapstick hits and falls seem twice as funny if they coincide with a well-timed bonk on a drum, wood-block or whatever is found to make the noise best suited to the action.

Pantomime demands a particular style of playing and production. The acting must be larger than life, but still sincere, with a good deal of sparkle and attack. Much of it must be projected directly at the audience, since one of pantomime's great advantages is that it deliberately breaks down the 'fourth wall'. The actors can literally and metaphorically shake hands with their audience who become almost members of the cast; indeed, their active participation from time to time is essential. A word of warning on this though, the actors must always remain

in control; they must never encourage a response to such an extent
that they can no longer be heard. This is particularly so in the case
of hissing; The OLD MAN OF THE SEA must take care that his every
appearance is not drowned in a sea of hisses or much of the effect of
his part - and much of the plot,too - will be lost; and the plot of a
pantomime is of prime importance because the larger part of the
audience, the children, like stories and like to be able to follow them.
Therefore the producer should ensure that the story line is clearly
brought out. This is especially necessary with a less well known
pantomime subject such as SINBAD THE SAILOR. In the 'Thousand
and One Nights' it is a collection of seven voyages,each of which
tells a separate story, which would be rather cumbersome for dramatic purposes. Consequently I have combined elements from the
various voyages to tell just one tale which - while remaining essen-
tially pantomime - should also be treated as something of an adventure story.

Teamwork is very necessary in pantomime so every member of the
cast should allow whoever has the important bit in a scene to be the
focus of attention. The selfish actor continually hogging the limelight
is distracting to the audience and very aggravating to the rest of the
cast! There is always room for local gags and topical quips in pantomime but they should not be overdone; nor should any of the comedy -
too much 'milking' of something the cast think is hilarious but the
audience obviously does not can slow down the pace disastrously - and
much of this script should go at a pretty spanking pace. It should also
be appreciated that any comedy scene needs rhythm and a shape; a
big laugh in the wrong place can upset the balance and actually make
the sequence as a whole less funny. Last, but certainly not least, the
comedy must never appear to be conscious of its own funniness.

Characterization should be clear and definite. I prefer the traditional
use of a man to play the Dame and a girl to play the Principal Boy. In
the case of the Dame, anyway, there is a sound argument for this;
audiences will laugh more readily at a man impersonating a woman
involved in the mock cruelties of slapstick than at a real woman. For
this reason an actor playing a Dame should never quite let us forget
he is a man while giving a sincere character performance of a
woman; further, he can be as feminine as he likes-but never effeminate

MRS SINBAD is a kindly, motherly soul. She takes life as she finds it
and, on the whole, finds it to be fun.

Like the Dame a Principal Boy also requires a character performance,
but with the implications reversed, of course! An occasional slap of
the thigh is not enough. SINBAD is cheeky, adventurous, resourceful
and plucky enough to deal with any situation into which these three

qualities lead him.

Principal Girls can be a bore, but only if they are presented as mere pretty symbols of feminine sweetness. YASMIN may be beautiful, but she also has a lot of guts and is clever, shrewd and humorous.

TINBAD is a model of devotion in his attachment to MRS SINBAD. He is funny, but not by intent. He regards himself as rather serious-minded but, of course, it is that which others find funny.

The PERI is as swift as quicksilver – both in thought and action. In appearance she should be glamorously exotic.

Her opponent, The OLD MAN OF THE SEA, should be played with a great deal of relish. He is single-minded in his dedication to evil and obviously desires to be the definitive personification of the man we love to hate.

ALI WHEY, though incompetent, does have some idea of what he's supposed to be about; his partner in crime, BAK ALI, is an ebullient fantasiser and is generally unconcerned with reality until, that is, a situation threatens to become dangerous, then he swiftly becomes a very realistic coward.

DRUSILA is a mischievous animal, but not malicious, and typical of her breed in that she is wayward and supercilious, but atypical in her addiction to laughter.

If necessary the CALIPH OF BAGDAD, BLACKBEARD THE GIANT, the SLAVE MASTER and the KHEDIVE OF EGYPT can all be played by one person. The characters have one trait in common - authority. Apart from that the CALIPH is a ruler much aware of his own importance and completely convinced of the rightness of his opinions; BLACKBEARD thinks himself to be uproarious, a point of view his captives do not share particularly as he looks terrifying; the SLAVE MASTER is also formidable and unused to argument, either from his slaves or anybody else, but is not without a certain sardonic sense of humour; the KHEDIVE, though not basically an unkind man, is so used to getting his own way that we feel if he did not get it the results would be very unpleasant.

It is also possible to double the KHEDIVE'S VIZIER and KING SERENDIB. The former is obviously an enigmatic character, while the latter is not called upon to display more than apparent age and agitation.

There can, of course, be as many or as few CHORUS and CHILDREN as desired.

JOHN CROCKER

PERI   Brass bottle
TINBAD   Guide book
DRUSILA   Loot bag
PERI   Doll replica of OLD MAN OF THE SEA

Off L

Boo-boo bird, on stick, to be pushed on.

TINBAD Umbrella CHECK

'SPECIAL INSTRUCTIONS'

SCENE 1   **PART I**

Brass bottle and   The bottle is made with a hole in its base. The
Dromedary milk   churn is set in front of an opening in the R wing
churn   which corresponds to a gap in the back of the
                    churn. The churn has a hole in its top. From
                    behind the wing a cane is pushed up through the
                    two holes and moved from side to side to make
                    the bottle wobble.

SCENE 3   PART I

Oven   The back of the oven is made of two overlapping
                    pieces of black material attached to the galley
                    backing. The sides and the top are hardboard on
                    2 x 1 frames hinged to the galley backing. The
                    front is a practical door in a 2 x 1 frame, which
                    is pin-hinged to the sides and the pins of the pin-
                    hinges are stapled to the oven top. The top and
                    sides have nylon lines fed through the galley
                    backing to be pulled when the explosion occurs.
                    The top being pulled up will release the pin-hinges,
                    the sides will be pulled outwards and the front will
                    fall of its own accord.

SCENE 5   PART I
and SCENES 1 & 3 PART II

Flying cut-outs   Three fine nylon lines will need to be stretched
                    across the top of the cyclorama like three separate
                    monorails. The cut-outs are hooked over these lines.
                    Attached to the front of each cut-out is another
                    nylon thread, the further end of which is threaded
                    over a pulley to pull the cut-out in whichever

<u>Off R</u>

SLAVE MASTER   Purse

<u>Off L</u>

DRUSILA   Rope halter
TINBAD   Filled sacks
BAK ALI   Watch
ALI WHEY   Handkerchief
MRS SINBAD   Plastic carrier bag containing twelve purses
ALI WHEY   Bag, labelled 'LOOT'
BAK ALI   Scissors

<u>Personal</u>

SLAVE MASTER   Whip
TINBAD Umbrella CHECK

<u>SCENE 2</u>
<u>Off R</u>

ALI WHEY   False moustache
BAK ALI   Joke teeth
ALI WHEY Loot Bag CHECK
TINBAD Umbrella CHECK

<u>SCENE 3</u>   Set onstage

In front of R wing: Pile of cushions
                   Hookah, with Government Health Warning label

<u>Off L</u>

TINBAD   Arab flute with bulbous end (see 'Special Instruc-
                   tions')
TINBAD   Hand drum

OLD MAN   Three small carpets

<u>SCENE 4</u>

<u>Off L</u>

                   Three magic carpet frames (see 'Special Instruc-
                   tions') for OLD MAN OF THE SEA & YASMIN,
                   SINBAD, and MRS SINBAD & TINBAD
MRS SINBAD   Policewoman's cap
TINBAD   Policeman's cap
TINBAD   Umbrella, with flashing blue light

<u>SCENE 5</u>   Set onstage

On rockpiece L: Fragment of YASMIN's dress material
In C :   Old log

FURNITURE AND PROPERTY PLOT

PART I

SCENE 1   Set onstage

In front of R wing: Broom
Milk churn labelled 'CAMEL'S MILK' with two
humps on its side
Milk churn labelled 'DROMEDARY'S MILK' with
one hump on its side. (see 'Special Instructions')

In front of L wing: Large roll of cloth with neatly rolled umbrella
inside it.

Off R

MRS SINBAD	Four-wheeled milk float with strap across front of shafts
SINBAD	Fishing rod and line
MRS SINBAD	Milk pail, costume concealed inside it

Off L

CALIPH	Letter
TINBAD	Enrobed Tailor's Dummy with card 'THE ROYAL LOOK'
TINBAD	Card 'GOING CHEAP'

Brass bottle (see 'Special Instructions') to be
attached to end of SINBAD's line
Identical Tailor's Dummy without robe in pose -
'September Morn'

To be dropped from flies in front of L wing a purse inscribed
'TINBAD'

SCENE 2

Off R

BAK ALI	Sherbert fountain

Personal

OLD MAN	Stick
ALI WHEY	Sword
BAK ALI	Sword

SCENE 3   Set onstage

In galley UC: On shelf - pie dish
Kitchen table, on it:- mixing bowl, sieve, rolling pin, jug of water, packet of flour, packet of
salt, concealed pieces of papier-maché, slab of
ready-made pastry.

                              Oven (see 'Special Instructions')

Off R

TINBAD   Box of pomegranates
BAK ALI   Box of bombs, similar looking to pomegranates
PERI   Charm on chain

Off L

DRUSILA   Rope halter
DRUSILA   Cloak, on one side in large childlike letters 'SHH!
                    I'M INVIZIBLE'
DRUSILA   Tray, with rope attached, small sign on tray,
                    'HEAR'
BAK ALI   Large club
CHORUS   Swords
                    Cannon ball, to be thrown on.
To ascend in C, or descend from flies - a dummy microphone
To fall from flies - the charred remains of the pie

Personal

SINBAD   **Sword**
BAK ALI   **Canary**
          TINBAD Umbrella CHECK

SCENE 4

Off L

OLD MAN   Crystal ball, bouncing
OLD MAN   Coil of rope
          TINBAD Umbrella CHECK

SCENE 5   Set onstage
                    Piles of very large diamonds
                    On L wing on pivoting arm - a rope

Off R

PIGMIES   Spears

Off L

SINBAD   Sack
TINBAD   Rope
MRS SINBAD   Two sacks
          TINBAD Umbrella   CHECK

PART II
SCENE 1   Set onstage

In front of L wing: Large sack, labelled 'BIRD SEED'

direction is required. The cut-outs in SCENE 5 are set, out of sight, from the beginning and struck in the interval to allow those for PART II, SCENES 1 and 3, to be set.

SCENE 3	PART II
Arab flute	The stem is made of two rigid pieces of tubing joined by a flexible piece. The flexible piece is kept rigid by a sliding tube which is moved down when the flute has to bend.

SCENE 4	PART II
Magic carpet frames	1. OLD MAN OF THE SEA & YASMIN 2. SINBAD 3. MRS SINBAD & TINBAD

Rectangular frames are covered and painted to look like carpets. In no. 2 there is one hole and in nos. 1 and 3 two holes for the artistes to fit into. Attached to the rims of these holes are shoulder straps to suspend the frames to about the tops of the artistes' thighs. At the front of each hole and fixed to the 'carpet' covering are kneeling or seated mock-ups of the limbs of the artiste concerned. Their own legs are concealed by the ground-row.

EFFECTS PLOT

PART I

SCENE 3

1.	tape	MRS SINBAD's voice, much amplified, saying: 'POMEGRANATE PIE'
2.	tape	Two loud splashes
3.	tape/maroon	Explosion
4.	tape/maroon	Cannon boom
5.	spot	Loud thump
6.	tape	Wind, thunder - storm continues into SCENE 4

SCENE 5

7.	tape	OLD MAN OF THE SEA's laughter on echo
8.	tape	SINBAD's voice on echo saying 'HELP'
9.	tape	SINBAD's voice louder and echoing round hill-sides saying 'HELP'
10.	tape	Thunderous footsteps
11.	tape	Flapping wings and crow-like croaking, much amplified

12.	tape	Croaking and flapping wings fading away

PART II   SCENE 1

13.	tape	Flapping wings approaching
14.	tape	Croaking
15.	tape	Single croak and wings flapping away

SCENE 3

16.	tape	Opening bars of Beethoven's 5th Symphony
17.	tape	Wailing flute ending with 'raspberry'

SCENE 4

18.	tape	Police siren
19.	spot	Loud bump off L
20.	spot	Second loud bump off L

SCENE 5

21.	tape	Several birds overhead crying 'Boo-boo'
22.	tape	Single bird overhead crying 'Boo-boo'

MUSIC PLOT

PART I

1.	OVERTURE	Orchestra

SCENE 1

2.	The Persian Scene	TINBAD & CHORUS
3.	SINBAD's entrance music	Orchestra
4.	Adventure	SINBAD & CHILDREN
5.	DRUSILA's music	Orchestra
6.	MRS SINBAD's music	Orchestra
7.	You Understand Me So Well	MRS SINBAD & TINBAD
8.	CALIPH's entrance music	Orchestra
9.	Catch Me	YASMIN & SINBAD
10a.	Bottle Wobble	Orchestra
10b.	Bottle wobble	Orchestra
11.	PERI's music	Orchestra
12.	PERI's exit, reprise 11	Orchestra
13	Let's Go	ENSEMBLE
	(continue, Orchestra only, as link to next scene and segue into cue 14)	

SCENE 2

14.	OLD MAN OF THE SEA's music	Orchestra
15.	ALI WHEY's entrance music	Orchestra
16.	Running music	Orchestra
17.	Nautical and Naughty	OLD MAN, ALI WHEY
	(continue, Orchestra only, as link to next scene and segue into cue 18)	& BAK ALI

45.	Flying carpet music	Orchestra
46.	Strobe chase music	Orchestra
	(continue as link to next scene and segue into cue 47)	

SCENE 4

47.	Rushing and falling music	Orchestra
48.	Dromedary	MRS SINBAD &
	(continue, orchestra only, as scene link)	Audience

SCENE 5

49.	Monkey Dance	CHILDREN
50.	Without Him	YASMIN
51.	PERI's music reprise 11	Orchestra
52.	Lesser Spotted Centipede music	Orchestra
53.	Shrinking music	Orchestra
54.	Baghdad!	ENSEMBLE
	(continue, orchestra only, as link to next scene)	

SCENE 6

55.	Don't You?	MRS SINBAD & TINBAD

SCENE 7

56.	Walk-down music, reprise 4	Orchestra
57.	Grand Finale	The Whole Company

SINBAD THE SAILOR

MUSIC 1   Overture

PART 1 SCENE 1   The Port of Balsora

Fullset. The rostrum represents a raised quayside, on the L of
which is a large capstan. A wing R bears the sign MRS SINBAD'S
CAMEL AND DROMER DAIRY, outside which stand a broom and two
large milk churns, one labelled CAMEL'S MILK (with two humps on
its side) and the onstage one DROMEDARY'S MILK (with one hump
on its side). A wing L carries the sign M. TINBAD TAILOR - NATTY
NAUTICALS FOR SAUCY SAILORS. Leaning against the wing is a
large roll of cloth with a neatly rolled umbrella inside it.

The CHORUS as townsfolk and street traders and the CHILDREN, as
street urchins, are on stage, their action frozen in silhouette. The
light come slowly up to reach their peak as the music simultaneously
builds to a crescendo and everybody springs into life. Enter TINBAD
from his shop L. Rather incongruously he wears a bowler hat.

MUSIC 2   The Persian Scene

TINBAD   If you're looking at our scenery,
                   And wonder where we're at,
               We've transported you to Persia,
                   And there's 'Welcome' on the mat.
               All these splendours architectural
                   Of a very foreign clime
               We've constructed out of cardboard
                   For a Persian Pantomime.

CHORUS   Yashmak - no mac -

TINBAD   Take a car and park it
                   In a Persian Market

CHORUS   Baa baa baksheesh -

TINBAD   There's a great elation
                   On location.

ALL   Though we went to school quite locally,

SINBAD THE SAILOR

Though abroad we've rarely been,
Now we're strictly middle-eastern,
Now we're in the Persian scene.

(Dance)

CHORUS   Salaam - purdah -

TINBAD   It is very trendy
                  If you say 'Effendi'.

CHORUS   Baghdad - good - bad -

TINBAD   It's a very hairy
                  Dictionary.

ALL   Though our only foreign travel
                  Has been to the Isle of Wight,
              With our Magic Carpet Package
                  We're in Persia for tonight.

              (The CHORUS are now in two groups, one L and
              one R, and the CHILDREN in a third group C.
              TINBAD picks up the roll of cloth and holds it on
              crooked forearms.)

L GROUP   (bowing) Greetings, O Tinbad the Tailor.

TINBAD   (bowing back) Oh, ta.

L GROUP   (bowing) May your days be long.

TINBAD   (bowing back) Well, the evenings are drawing out.

L GROUP   (bowing) And may all your burdens be light.

TINBAD   (bowing back) I wish this one was.

L GROUP   (bowing especially low) Salaam.

TINBAD   (bowing equally low) Salaam. (drops roll of
              cloth on feet and his bowler falls off) Ow!

              (L GROUP exit as TINBAD starts to pick up cloth)

R GROUP   (bowing) Greetings, O Tinbad.

TINBAD   Oh, not the whole lot again!

R GROUP   (bowing) Salaam.

TINBAD   Thank goodness for that. Sa- ah! (puts roll of
              cloth vertically in front of him with one end on

the floor) Salaam! (bows and bangs his chin on
the top of the roll)   OW!

(R GROUP exit. CHILDREN giggle and nudge each
other as he picks up cloth again.)

CHILD 1   O highly respected Tinbad the Tailor.

TINBAD   Yes, O scruffiest of street urchins?

CHILD 1   (bowing) Salaam!

TINBAD   (looks at roll of cloth and tucks it under his arm)
               Salaam. (bows and bangs his face on the end of
               the roll sticking out in front of him) Ow!

               (CHILDREN laugh and run off.)

               Rather painful these old Persian customs. Still
               you have to do it here, so - (bows to audience)
               Salaam! (looks at them and bows again) Salaam!
               I have to go on doing this till you say 'Salaam'
               back to me. Don't worry, it's not rude, it just
               means peace. (bows) Salaam! (audience reac-
               tion) That's better. It's a sort of neighbourly
               gesture, you see. But perhaps you haven't met
               your neighbours. Well, everybody say 'Salaam'
               to the people on your right - now to the people on
               your left. Very good, but why did you keep turning
               your backs on each other? It's lucky you're down
               there in (locality of show). It's a deadly insult
               up here in Persia. I can explain these things to
               you because I am practically English - my great-
               great-grandmother nearly married an Englishman.
               (replaces bowler and takes umbrella from the roll
               of cloth) It still shows though, doesn't it? Well
               now, today I'm going to make my fortune. I've
               got to, I'm completely impecunious. That's Persian
               for skint.   Not a sequin to my name. That's our
               kind of money here, sequins, but I haven't got any.
               Well, you can't ask a woman to marry you in that
               condition. Oh, I know I shouldn't. I know it's only
               twenty tiny years since we met, but I always was
               a mad, impetuous fool. Ah, dear little - little -
               I must find out her first name before I propose.
               I'm going to make my fortune with this. (indicates
               roll of cloth) That's a royal robe for the Caliph

SINBAD THE SAILOR

of Baghdad, that is. Well, it will be if I get to him before anybody else, and I should be able to because - (looks round cautiously) shall I let you into a secret?

(Some CHORUS look on round wings L and R.)

CHORUS   A secret? Yes!

TINBAD   (unaware of them) That's very good. I didn't see your lips move at all. Anyway, listen - he's coming here today - the Caliph of Baghdad!

CHORUS   The Caliph of Baghdad!

TINBAD   You did it again! I'll tell you something else - he's bringing his daughter with him.

CHORUS   The Princess Yasmin! (heads disappear)

TINBAD   Oh, you know her name. Come to think of it, I might be able to run up a little something for her too. But anyway, I'll be by Royal Appointment. I'll be made! People will come flocking -

(CHORUS enter L and R running to and fro whispering excitedly.)

There, they have already.

CHORUS   (whispers grow in volume) Have you heard? The Caliph of Baghdad! Coming to Balsora! This very day! His daughter, too! The Princess Yasmin! etc.

TINBAD   (to audience) Oh, you rotten lot, you've gone and told them.

CHORUS   (dispersing L and R) We must prepare for him! Our finest wares! Nothing but the best! etc.

(CHILDREN run on L.)

CHILDREN   Mr Tinbad!

CHILD 2   Have you heard the Caliph of Baghdad's coming today?

TINBAD   Oh, Persian fiddlesticks! (stalks into his shop)

CHILD 3 (a girl)   No, it's true, Mr Tinbad.

CHILD 4   And he's bringing the beautiful Princess Ysmin.

CHILD 5   The most beautiful girl in all Persia.

TINBAD   (looking out) The second most beautiful girl.
                  The most beautiful is little - little - I'll let you
                  know. (disappears from sight)

CHILD 6   Let's tell Sinbad!

CHILDREN   (rushing R) Yes, Sinbad! Sinbad! Sinbad!

SINBAD   (off - behind capstan L) Hullo, I'm over here.

CHILDREN   (turning) Where?

SINBAD   Here!

MUSIC 3   SINBAD's Entrance

                  (He enters from behind capstan, with fishing rod.
                  CHILDREN cluster round shouting his name.)

                  Shh! Not so loud! Mother might hear. She
                  wants me to do something or other.

CHILD 1   What?

SINBAD   I don't know. If I'd stayed to find out I might
                  have had to do it and I want to go fishing.

CHILD 2   But aren't you going to wait and see the Caliph?

CHILD 3   And the Princess?

SINBAD   Well, I don't expect they'll want to see me so
                  why should I want to see them?

CHILD 3   Because - because - well, the Princess is
                  beautiful.

SINBAD   Maybe, but she's a girl.

GIRLS   What's wrong with girls?

SINBAD   They're soppy.

                  (GIRLS give an outraged shriek.)

                  And they squeak.

GIRLS   Ocooh!

SINBAD   And they're very easy to tease.

                  (BOYS laugh and GIRLS start to pummel SINBAD.)

                  Hold on! I didn't mean girls like you!

SINBAD THE SAILOR

GIRLS   (stopping) Ah!

SINBAD   I meant pretty girls.

GIRLS   Oh! (hitting him with renewed vigour)

SINBAD   I think I'll get on with my fishing. It's safer.

CHILD 4   Why do you like fishing so much, Sinbad?

CHILD 5   You hardly ever catch anything.

SINBAD   No, but it's a nice way to sit and look at the sea
            and dream I'm sailing on it. In fact, I'm just in
            the middle of a very exciting voyage. I've fought
            off some pirates and sunk their ship, but now a
            terrible storm's sprung up and I'm wondering
            whether or not to be shipwrecked.

CHILD 6   It doesn't sound very comfortable.

SINBAD   Comfortable? You can't expect adventures to be
            comfortable. But that's what I want - adventure.

MUSIC 4   Adventure

            Keep sitting by the fireside,
                Stay home and read your book,
            Be busy doing nothing -
                But for me, give me adventure.
            Sit watching television -
                It's easy just to look -
            Waste time with games and parties -
                But for me, give me adventure.

            Give me a ship, give me a road, give me a reason;
            My bags are packed, I'll travel whatever the season.
            So -
            I don't care what your choice is;
                You do the things you like.
            There's just one life for living,
                And for me, give me adventure.

            I know of places beyond the horizon,
                Wonderful places with cities of gold.
            I'm not afraid of the cold and the darkness,
                I'm cunning, I'm daring, I'm bold!

            Give me a ship, give me a road, give me a reason;
            My bags are packed, I'll travel whatever the season.

So -
I don't care what your choice is;
   You do the things you like.
There's just one life for living,
   And for me, give me adventure,
   Give me adventure,
   Give me adventure!

(SINBAD and CHILDREN exit L.)

MRS SINBAD   (off R) Drusila! Wait, you silly dromedary, wait!

MUSIC 5   DRUSILA's Entrance

(DRUSILA the dromedary scampers on R.)

(off) Drusila! Come back!

(DRUSILA shakes her head and runs off L.)

MUSIC 6   MRS SINBAD's Entrance

(MRS SINBAD runs on R, pushing against a strap
across the front of the shafts of a four-wheeled
milk float.)

Drusila, where are you?

(DRUSILA looks on L. MRS SINBAD stops in C.
The float, under its own momentum, continues
and buffets her in the behind - she is knocked
over. DRUSILA gives a high-pitched laugh and
re-enters. — DRUSILA's laugh throughout
can be enhanced by the use of a radio throat
microphone, if feasible—)

It's not funny, Drusila, it's caused a nasty
affront to my front.

(MRS SINBAD turns to face front, her bustle is
sticking out on the L side. DRUSILA laughs again
and points a foreleg at it.)

Now what are you laughing at? (looks down) Oh,
me old Persian bustle's slipped.

DRUSILA   (whispers in her ear)

MRS SINBAD   Drusila! I'm surprised at you! She's made a
naughty funny - she says I'm all behind this
morning.

SINBAD THE SAILOR

(MRS SINBAD adjusts her skirt and DRUSILA
starts to beat the floor in a paroxysm of mirth
at her own joke.)

Drusila, you're getting hysterical. Pull yourself together.

DRUSILA   (suddenly stops laughing and closes up her rear
half to her front)

MRS SINBAD   Not that much together. She gets all wound up
in herself, you know. Well, I'll have to unwind
her.

(MRS SINBAD turns DRUSILA's tail like a handle.
Ratchet noises from Drummer as DRUSILA jerks
herself back to the right shape.)

That's better. Now, I expect you've gathered
this is Drusila.

DRUSILA   (becomes rather coy)

MRS SINBAD   No, don't be shy, dear, just say how-do to
everybody.

DRUSILA   (curtseys to audience)

MRS SINBAD   Very nice; and I'm Mrs Sinbad. That's because
my husband was Mr Sinbad - and my son's called
Sinbad too. Of course, it runs in the family. Of course,
I've lost my poor dear husband, but he was a
lovely man - I think. I didn't know him very well,
he was away at sea so much. Still he seemed very
nice when he was at home. But now that boy of
mine wants to be a sailor. I want him to be a
milkman, then I wouldn't have to run around
pulling this thing. Mark you, Drusila's supposed
to do that, aren't you, Drusila?

DRUSILA   (looks around airily)

MRS SINBAD   Now don't pretend you don't know what I mean.
Off you go and get in there. After all, why keep
a dog if you have to bite yourself? That's an old
Persian proverb. Go on, Drusila, in you get.

DRUSILA   (moves unwillingly to the float then, when MRS
SINBAD's back is turned, looks at her mischie-
vously, and sits in the back of the float.)

MRS SINBAD	She always obeys me in the end, you know. (turns and sees DRUSILA) Drusila! You know I didn't mean in there. Stop being naughty.
DRUSILA	(jumps up and runs towards the front of float)
MRS SINBAD	That's right, and into the –
	(DRUSILA keeps on running and disappears into TINBAD's shop.)
	Drusila! Oh, the wicked girl. (picks up broom from outside her dairy) Just wait till she comes out! (waits outside shop door)
DRUSILA	(off – laughs)
	(MRS SINBAD raises the broom and buffets TINBAD with it, as he runs backwards out of the shop, and knocks him down.)
MRS SINBAD	(aghast) Mr Tinbad! Are you all right?
TINBAD	What? Where? Who? (rises and sees MRS SINBAD) Aah! (aside to audience) 'Tis she! My little – little – you know.
MRS SINBAD	I'm so sorry, Mr Tinbad.
TINBAD	Not at all, my pleasure – I mean, my fault. I should never have got in the way of your broom.
MRS SINBAD	I thought you were –
	(DRUSILA runs on from shop laughing.)
	Drusila!
	(She aims another blow at DRUSILA but again misses and hits TINBAD, while DRUSILA continues off R, delighted at the havoc she has caused.)
TINBAD	(still reeling) Silly me, I did it again.
MRS SINBAD	But I hit you. (puts broom aside)
TINBAD	I know. So kind of you; and it gives me a chance to tell you that I – I intend to press my suit.
MRS SINBAD	Well, after the way I've been knocking you about I'm sure it needs a good press. But let me press it for you.

SINBAD THE SAILOR

TINBAD	Oh no. I mean - I intend to press my suit with you.
MRS SINBAD	Ah, you'd like us to press it together.
TINBAD	Together? Oh, yes please - but not yet. I have to make my fortune first.
MRS SINBAD	Oh, I shouldn't wait that long. Your suit will be worn out. I should press it now.
TINBAD	No, I couldn't really. There's another reason. You see, Mrs Sinbad - er -
MRS SINBAD	Yes?
TINBAD	The truth is, Mrs Sinbad - er -
MRS SINBAD	Yes?
TINBAD	I don't know your name, Mrs Sinbad.
MRS SINBAD	You don't? Well, you've been guessing awfully well.
TINBAD	Ah, that's what I like about you - you understand me so well.
MRS SINBAD	Do I? Well, I never!
MUSIC 7	You Understand Me So Well

BOTH	One can sometimes meet someone
	And want to become one
	    With ev'ry thing they say or do.
	It is hard to achieve it,
	But - would you believe it! -
	    I think that that someone is you.

MRS SINBAD	You accept without blinking The thoughts I am thinking.
TINBAD	You seem to be able to tell -
MRS SINBAD	You are much too discreet to remark that I'm fat.
TINBAD	You blush when I tell you that I like your cat.
MRS SINBAD	And when I stand on one leg you don't stop to chat,
BOTH	'Cos you understand me so well.

	When I tell the Tax man
	I have gone to Japan
	    And I won't be back home till the fall,
	You can capture my mood
	And say I'm in Bermu -
	    -da the next time he happens to call.

TINBAD

If at times I may look in
To see what you're cookin',
    I'm quite overpowered by the smell.

MRS SINBAD

I'll prepare all your favourite food in a tick.
I must say, I don't say I'm good - but I'm quick!

TINBAD

And you don't bat an eye when I say 'I feel sick!'

BOTH

    'Cos you understand me,
    Yes, you understand me,
    'Cos you understand me so well!

(MRS SINBAD exits R with the milk float. TINBAD
stands staring after her - moonstruck.)

VOICES

(off L) Make way for the Caliph of Baghdad. Way
for the Caliph!

TINBAD

(jumping slightly) The Caliph! My big chance!
My robe! My fortune and my little - little - !

(As he runs off into the shop L CHORUS and
CHILDREN pour on excitedly chattering from L
followed by two CALIPH's GUARDS.)

GUARDS

Make way for the Caliph and the Princess Yasmin.

MUSIC 8

Entrance of the CALIPH

(CALIPH and PRINCESS YASMIN enter from L.)

CHORUS &
CHILDREN

(bowing) Salaam!

CALIPH & YASMIN

(bowing) Salaam!

CHORUS 1 (R)
CHORUS 2 (L)

Welcome, O mightiest of Monarchs! (bows)
And welcome, O sweetest of Princesses! (bows)

YASMIN

(aside to CALIPH) I don't feel very sweet.

CALIPH

(aside to YASMIN) Never mind, my child, just
look it in front of the populace.

(YASMIN fixes the most charming of smiles on
her face throughout the following.)

Greetings, O citizens of Balsora. This is a happy
day for me.

(The CHORUS gasps during which YASMIN's
remark is lost to them but not to the audience.)

YASMIN   But not for me.

CALIPH   And, my daughter assures me, for her also because today she sets sail for India.

                (CHORUS reaction.)

YASMIN   Which I don't want to do.   } together

CALIPH   Which, she tells me, delights her as her bride-groom is the fabulously wealthy King Serendib of India.

                (CHORUS reaction.)

YASMIN   Who's old enough to be my grandfather.   } together

CALIPH   Whom she is sure will make her the happiest of women, since she is marrying him for the best of reasons.

                (CHORUS reaction.)

YASMIN   The money.   } together

CALIPH   To please her father. May all of you be blest with such daughters.

                (CHORUS reaction.)

                If I have to suffer, why shouldn't they?   } together
                But now the Princess is anxious to board the noble craft which - (notices the empty harbour for first time) - which isn't there!

                (CHORUS gasps.)

YASMIN   Hurray!   } together

CALIPH   Shut up!
                Where is the Harbour-Master?

CHILD 1   Let me show you, Excellency.

CHILD 2   No, let me.

CALIPH   All right, you can both show me.

CHILD 1 & 2   This way, Excellency!

                (CHILD 2 runs off R and CHILD 1 runs off L.)

CALIPH   Somebody else show me!

CHORUS & CHILDREN	Yes, Excellency!
CALIPH	The quickest way.
CHORUS & CHILDREN	This way! (they exit L and R)
CALIPH	Idiots! Why am I surrounded by bungling fools? Some bungling fool obviously forgot to order the ship. Look - (produces a letter from pocket) here's the letter I wrote giving the order. So who's responsible, eh?
YASMIN	The bungling fool who left it in your pocket, father.
CALIPH	Precisely, the bungling fool who - well, anyway - I'll commandeer a ship. Guards, take me to the Harbour-Master.
GUARDS	Yes, Excellency.
	(GUARD 1 exits L and GUARD 2 exits R. The CALIPH, furious, starts to stride L and then R.)
YASMIN	How about eeny meeny miny mo?
CALIPH	Tcha!
	(He strides L again and bumps into TINBAD who enters from his shop carrying a richly clothed tailor's dummy, with a card on it 'The Royal Look'.)
	Out of my way, man!
TINBAD	But you got in my way. Who do you think you are?
CALIPH	The Caliph of Baghdad.
TINBAD	(gulps) You're right. I got in your way. So sorry. (indicates dummy) But what about this, eh?
CALIPH	What about it? If you want to play with life-size dolls that's your problem. Mine's the Harbour-Master. Where is he?
TINBAD	Ah, which way do you want to go? That way or that way?
CALIPH	Whichever way you're not going.

TINBAD	Oh, I'm not going the other way.
CALIPH	Good. (starts to move off L)
TINBAD	So I'll come with you. Now, about this robe -
	(They disappear L.)
YASMIN	I don't believe there is a Harbour-Master. I'll look this way.
	(She moves R and almost bumps into SINBAD as he enters there with a fishing rod over his DS shoulder.)
YASMIN & SINBAD	Sorry.
	(Both sidestep US.)
	Oh!
	(Both sidestep DS. They shrug and laugh and SINBAD indicates to her that she should go first. YASMIN exits R.)
SINBAD	I wonder who -
	(YASMIN re-enters, caught on the end of his line. - the end of line has been held off-stage on SIN- BAD's entrance to be hooked on to her dress -)
YASMIN	Well, this really is a new line.
SINBAD	What? Oh, sorry. (unhooks her) I'm afraid that was a bit of bad luck.
YASMIN	Oh dear, does that mean you're going to throw me back?
SINBAD	(laughs) No, I meant - well, perhaps it wasn't bad luck, rather good luck for me. My name's Sinbad, by the way, what's yours?
YASMIN	Yasmin.
SINBAD	That's nice. Just like the - oh! Perhaps you are the -
YASMIN	Which particular the?
SINBAD	The the.
YASMIN	That's me.
SINBAD	Oh. I've never met one before and yet, you're, well

YASMIN	Just like any other girl?
SINBAD	Yes - but more so. I'm not anybody or anything yet. I want to be a sailor, though, and one day I mean to have my own ship.
YASMIN	Well, don't get it too soon or you might have to take me to India to get married to King Serendib.
SINBAD	Married? Oh. (moves US) I wonder how the fish are here. (casts line to off L)
YASMIN	Much better without you trying to stick hooks in-to them. I don't want to get married, you know.
SINBAD	You don't? (moves DS, leaving rod on rostrum) I'm bored with fishing. But I suppose you will want to get married - sometime.
YASMIN	Sometime. But I don't want just to be given to somebody, I want to be -
SINBAD	Caught?
YASMIN	Hook, line and sinker.

MUSIC 9	Catch Me
	Catch me, catch me, catch me if you can. Prove you are a huntin', fishin' man. Somewhere off the shore-line I will make for your line, Then hook, line and sinker I will take your bait.
SINBAD	Catch you, catch you, catch you I will try; I've lots of tempting lures just standing by.
YASMIN	And if I must be landed, I can hardly wait, 'Cos I want to be caught by you.
SINBAD	'Cos you're bound to be caught by me. ⎫ together
YASMIN	Why are you specially fishing for me?
SINBAD	It's something compulsive to do.
YASMIN	There s plenty of other good fish in the sea -
SINBAD	But nothing as tasty as you!
YASMIN	Catch me, etc (repeat)....... ...'Cos I want to be caught -
SINBAD	You're bound to be caught.

YASMIN	I want to be caught by you.
SINBAD	You're bound to be caught by me.

together

(YASMIN exits R. TINBAD enters L wailing loudly, with the dummy which he dumps down and puts a scrawled card 'GOING CHEAP' on it.)

SINBAD What's the matter, Mr Tinbad?

TINBAD Oh, Sinbad, I'm ruined, ruined! No sale, no fortune, no little - little -

SINBAD Little little?

TINBAD Yes, your, your - is my little, little. But not now, because all that Caliph wants is a ship. That's all he talked about - a ship. On and on, a ship, a ship, a ship. What does he expect me to do - run him up a three-piece yacht in mohair? Ruined! Ruined! (runs off into his shop)

SINBAD Well, I want a ship, too, but even more now I want - well, I don't expect I'll be able to find anybody to help me get either. (picks up rod) Hullo, I've got a bite.

(MRS SINBAD enters R holding a milk pail under DRUSILA. Costume concealed in pail.)

MRS SINBAD Drusila, stand still, I can't milk you on the trot. Oh, Sinbad, there you are, you naughty boy. Come and help me with Drusila.

SINBAD Hold on, Mother, I've got a bite - a big bite.

MRS SINBAD You mean we're having tiddlers for tea again?

SINBAD No, really big. It's coming - look! (draws in a dirty old brass bottle on the end of line) Oh!

(DRUSILA kills herself with laughter and runs off. MRS SINBAD puts pail down UC.)

MRS SINBAD Strange sense of humour that animal. Just because all you catch is an old bottle -

SINBAD But it's not an ordinary old bottle.

MRS SINBAD A very ordinary old bottle that -

SINBAD It's an old brass bottle.

MRS SINBAD	A very ordinary old brass bottle that - a brass bottle! I've read about that sort of thing. Sinbad, we're rich! Give it to me, I know how to deal with it.
	(SINBAD gives her the bottle and she puts it down on the Dromedary milk churn - see Special Instructions.)
	Now watch. I just rub it gently and .... just rub it a bit harder and ... (knocks on side of bottle) Oy! Wake up in there! I rub it very hard and... Useless! Silly boy, you've been fishing in the wrong story. Chuck it back. (exits R)
SINBAD	Seems a pity. It looks quite interesting. Still, maybe she's right. I will chuck it back.
MUSIC 10a	(As he goes to pick it up the bottle starts to wobble: Bottle Wobble)
	That's odd.
MUSIC 10b	(It stops. He puts a hand out towards it and it wobbles again. Bottle Wobble)
	Very odd. It's heavily sealed, too. There must be something inside it. (to audience) Do you think I should open it? (audience reaction) Do you? (audience reaction) You do! (prising it open) It's not too easy, but I think I'm getting it - there! (looks expectantly at bottle) Nothing. Nothing at -
MUSIC 11	(A drum roll starts - lights flicker. SINBAD backs away to hide behind the capstan. Drum roll ends with a mighty cymbal crash. Blackout. White flash R and lights up to reveal the PERI. PERI Music (SINBAD peers fearfully over top of capstan.)
	Coo!
PERI	Coo? (goes into peals of delicious laughter) That's all you say - just coo?
SINBAD	Well - is your name Drusila,too?
PERI	(finds this even more funny - shakes her head) I laugh'd because 'coo' seem'd absurd,

SINBAD THE SAILOR

        Yet it's the sweetest sound I've heard
        Within a thousand years. You see
        It's all that long since I've been free.

SINBAD   You mean - in there?

PERI   That's been my home
        With very little space to roam;
        And as that bottle's rather damp,
        A thousand years I've had the cramp.
        Can I still run - and leap - and whirl?
        (suits actions to the words)
        I can!

SINBAD   I'll say! You're quite a girl.

PERI   I'm not a girl, I'm called a Peri.

SINBAD   What, like a Genie?

PERI   No, not very;
        Genies obey, at least they should,
        We Peris, though, are pledg'd to good.
        The choice is ours, though, what to do.
        So I shall choose some good for you.
        You want to be a sailor?

SINBAD   Yes.

PERI   And win the Princess?

SINBAD   How d'you guess?

PERI   Ah, I all mortal thoughts can read.
        Now, as a sailor, your first need
        Will be a ship. That's not too hard.
        It's where ships sail that's rather jarr'd.

SINBAD   Why?

PERI   He who there imprison'd me
        Is called the Old Man of the Sea,
        An evil creature through and through,
        He'll want revenge on me - and you -
        And out at sea the peril's more.

SINBAD   I'd rather that than stay on shore.

PERI   Well, some protection I can grant.
        So now your ship.

SINBAD   You mean....? You can't!

PERI

I can, unless my magic's rusty.
But first, your clothes look - (shrugs)

SINBAD

                              Rather dusty?

PERI

Well, something smarter might be wise
For Captain's wear. Try this for size.

(She makes magic pass at the dummy. A single
note tings on a bell and the lights blackout. The
dummy is whisked away and replaced by a dummy
stripped of robes and in a 'September Morn'
position. PERI takes concealed costume from
pail, lights come up to reveal stripped dummy
and PERI holding coat.)

Will this style suit you? (throws coat to SINBAD)

SINBAD

                          Will it ? Coo! (exits L)

PERI

Now. two more magic tasks to do -
A purse to make peace with the Tailor!

(She makes a magic pass at TINBAD's door.
There is a 'ting' and a purse inscribed TINBAD
drops in front of it from above.)

A ship to make Sinbad a sailor!

MUSIC 12

PERI Music   (exit PERI R)

TINBAD

(entering from shop) What was that? A purse!
(picks it up) It's got my name on it - and it's
full of gold sequins! But what - where - who?
Of course! The Caliph! He's changed his mind.

CALIPH

(entering R) Ridiculous! Not a single ship. Not
even a paddle boat.

TINBAD

(bowing) Your Caliphness.

CALIPH

Oh, go away.

TINBAD

But, sire, the robe you paid for -

CALIPH

Are you still jabbering on about robes?

TINBAD

Yes, sire, and I'm sure you'll never look better
than dressed like this. (moves stripped dummy
between them)

CALIPH

WHAT!

TINBAD (notices the state of the dummy, gulps in horrified astonishment, then whips the dummy away) So sorry. Slight mistake. (hurrying off to shop) You naughty dummy, get back in the shop. (ventriloquising) It's not my fault. (normal voice) Shut up! (exit)

CALIPH Idiot! Keeps on about robes when all I want is a ship. It's absurd. The biggest port in my kingdom and -

(Lights start to dim as PERI enters UR on rostrum making magic passes to offstage.)

Hmm, sudden storm.... As I was saying -

(Drum roll starts as cut-out of 'The Sublime Sultana' slides on.)

How dare it thunder when I'm talking? I know I'm only talking to myself, but how can I hear myself? I might say something interesting.

(Drum roll ends and the lights come up.)

Ah, I see the elements know their place. Where was I? Oh yes, a ship.

(PERI taps him on shoulder. He flicks at his shoulder as if brushing away a fly.)

Or rather, no ship.

(PERI taps his other shoulder with the same result. She shrugs, moves US and makes magic passes L and R. Each pass is punctuated by a 'ting' and PERI becomes increasingly frustrated by the CALIPH's lack of observation - ting.)

Beastly place is fly-ridden. But I want a -

GUARDS (running on L and R) A ship! A ship!

CALIPH Exactly. But there isn't one. (ting) So where can I get a -

MRS SINBAD & (runs on R⎞
TINBAD (runs on L⎠ A ship! A ship!

CALIPH It's no use everybody just saying that. (ting) It doesn't give me a -

CHORUS & CHILDREN	(running on L and R) A ship! A ship!
CALIPH	I keep telling you, there isn't a ship.
ALL	(pointing US) There is!
CALIPH	(to audience) There isn't, is there? (audience reaction) No need to whisper. Well - (turns US) There is! How did that get there? Never mind, where's the captain?
	(PERI gestures R . There's a ting and SINBAD enters dressed in coat from dummy. Exit PERI R.)
SINBAD	(bowing) Salaam!
ALL	Sinbad!
CALIPH	Ah, Captain Sinbad, eh?
MRS SINBAD	(aside) Sinbad, what's happened?
SINBAD	(aside) The bottle.
MRS SINBAD	(aside) Oh, and you so young!
SINBAD	(aside) The brass bottle, Mother!
CALIPH	Captain Sinbad, I commandeer your ship to take my daughter to her future husband.
SINBAD	To her future husband? Delighted. I agree. (bows)
YASMIN	(entering L) But I don't.
	(SINBAD looks up and winks at her, she gasps.)
	I do!
	(Everyone cheers.)
CALIPH	Women! Well, that's settled -
MRS SINBAD	Not quite. If my son's going, so am I.
TINBAD	Then so am I. (reaches into shop for bowler hat and umbrella)
CHORUS & CHILDREN	And us!
CALIPH	Anybody else? (DRUSILA runs on R wearing a sailor hat) Hm. Should be good for a laugh.
	(DRUSILA is offended and stalks off to exit by ship.)

I - 1 - 22   SINBAD THE SAILOR

              If that's the lot, then off to sea!
ALL   Off to sea!
MUSIC 13   Let's Go!

              Heave ho! Let's Go!
                  Set the mizzen spanker;
                  Yank aloft the anchor.
              Cast off! Blast off!
                  You can all be sharing
                  Our seafaring.
              All this busy to and froing
                  Means at last we're under way.
              Off to foreign parts we're going
                  Our adventure starts today.

              BLACKOUT

              (Close traverse tabs. Fly in Scene 2 frontcloth.)

I - 2 - 22   SCENE 2 The Cave of the OLD MAN OF THE SEA

              (During scene open tabs when ready to reveal a
              rather murky looking rocky frontcloth. In front of
MUSIC 14   tabs a green flash L. OLD MAN Music as he leaps
              clumsily on L, hampered by a bulbously bandaged
              R foot. He carries a stick.)

OLD MAN   Powers of evil, come to my aid!
              Something nasty my day's unmade!
              That Peri's out and seeks for me
              For I'm the Old Man of the Sea!
              Ooh, stop! No, you don't make me cringe,
              It's just me gout's begun to twinge.
              I'm not scared by boos and hisses,
              So same to you with love and kisses! (pulls face)
              That Peri, though - well, what's she for?
              Why - goodness! That to me means war!
              I search for it and stamp it out! (stamps)
              OW! Help! Rude words! Forgot me gout!
              Ah well, that painful little dance
              Has cost the Peri her last chance;
              Young Sinbad too, the silly duffer,
              With Ma and sweetheart - all shall suffer!

This pesky foot, though, cuts my speed,
Help with the leg work's what I need.
(looking off R)
Hullo, who's this that comes this way?
Two likely villains I should say.
They're doubtless up to dirty work,
To find out what - I'll have a lurk. (exit L)

MUSIC 15	(ALI WHEY's Entrance He enters R with elaborate caution, stopping after a few steps with a finger to his lips.)
ALI WHEY	Ssh! (advances another few steps and turns back) Ssh! (reaches C, stops and looks all round with a hand shielding his eyes) All right, all clear, but ssh!
	(Loud shouts off R and BAK ALI enters noisily and energetically fighting the air with his sword.)
	Shut up! Stop it! What are you doing?
BAK ALI	(momentarily stopping) Fighting. (carries on)
ALI WHEY	Fighting? Fighting who? There's nobody there.
BAK ALI	(stopping again) I know. It's much safer that way. (adds a final lunge or two and sheathes his sword) I won!
ALI WHEY	Idiot! Nobody one.
BAK ALI	Did he? That's the last time I fight him then. (suddenly clutches his breast and staggers round with a few agonising cries before subsiding to the ground)
ALI WHEY	Now what are you doing?
BAK ALI	Nothing. I'm deaded.
ALI WHEY	Get up! You're not deaded - I mean dead, because there's nobody here to deaded - to dead, to er- well, anyway there isn't. Is that clear?
BAK ALI	Not very, you got a bit muddled with your deadeds.
ALI WHEY	All right, I'll put it another way. I'm here. You know who I am, don't you?
BAK ALI	Yes. Don't you?

ALI WHEY	Of course I do. Who am I?
BAK ALI	You just said you knew.
ALI WHEY	Answer the question. Who am I?
BAK ALI	Ali Whey.
ALI WHEY	And who are you?
BAK ALI	Bak Ali.
ALI WHEY	Right; and as we're here all by ourselves, what does it mean?
BAK ALI	Nobody loves us?
ALI WHEY	No! It means we're the only ones who are here. There's nobody beside us.
BAK ALI	Oh, is he back? (draws sword) I'll get him this time.
ALI WHEY	Put that away! All I mean is, there is no other single person here. Got it?
BAK ALI	Got it. You mean all that lot out there are married.
ALI WHEY	Ye- no! I mean - well, they're not really there.
BAK ALI	Aren't they?
ALI WHEY	No. (turning away) Now let me see -
BAK ALI	(to audience) You're not ther-ere. (audience reaction) Oh no, you're no-ot. (audience reaction) Oh no, you're not! (audience reaction) Oh no, you're not! (audience reaction) You're not, you're not, you're not! (audience reaction) Not-not-not-not-not-NOT! (audience reaction) What are you laughing at? Pom-tiddley-om-pom! (pulls face - audience reacts) I think they are there, you know.
ALI WHEY	You're making things very awkward. Of course they are there - but they're not to us, though we are to them. It's all a question of imagination.
BAK ALI	You mean we're just imagining them?
ALI WHEY	No, but in a way they're imagining us. You could say we're just figments of their imagination.

BAK ALI	Figments? I don't want to be a figment. If I have to be a figment I don't want to play.
ALI WHEY	Listen, Bak, what are we doing here?
BAK ALI	Figmenting.
ALI WHEY	No. we re smuggling. And what are we smuggling? Sherbert.
BAK ALI	I like sherbert.
ALI WHEY	I know, and that's why we're stuck with a load of it. Let's smuggle sherbert, you said. And what did we find? Sherbert, bags of it, all over Baghdad. They've even got sherbert fountains!
BAK ALI	So have I. (produces one) Want a suck?
ALI WHEY	No, put it away. Well, we'll just have to stache all our sherbert and wait for a sherbert shortage. Meanwhile we'll have to do something else. But what?
OLD MAN	(leaping on L) Aha!
ALI WHEY & BAK ALI	Waah.
MUSIC 16	(Running Music ALI WHEY starts to run off R. BAK ALI catches hold of his collar and also starts to run.)
BAK ALI	Don't leave me!
	(OLD MAN OF THE SEA hooks his stick in BAK ALI s collar so that he and ALI WHEY are held running on the spot.)
OLD MAN	Surely you're not frightened by an old man like me?
BAK ALI	Why not? We're not fussy. We're frightened by anybody.
OLD MAN	Pity. I wanted to make you rich.
ALI WHEY & BAK ALI	Rich? (they stop running)
ALI WHEY	We re not frightened.
OLD MAN	Then why were you running?

SINBAD THE SAILOR

ALI WHEY   Er -

BAK ALI   Exercise. We like to keep fit. (starts jumping
                  legs astride and flinging arms out and in) Out -
                  in! Out - in! Out - in! Out - in! Out - in!
                  Out -

OLD MAN   OW! (BAK ALI lands on gouty foot) ⎫ together
                  You fool!   ⎭

BAK ALI   (sliding round to other side of ALI WHEY) Yes,
                  control yourself, Ali.

ALI WHEY   But I -

OLD MAN   Never mind. Now you're seafaring men, so
                  what about a little piracy and slave-trading?

ALI WHEY   Right up our street.

OLD MAN   Good. Then I want you to take off just three
                  slaves. But I'll pay well for them. Ten thousand
                  sequins.

ALI WHEY   Ten thousand sequins!

BAK ALI   Ah, 'Come Dancing' here we come.

ALI WHEY   Where do we find these slaves?

OLD MAN   Aboard the 'Sublime Sultana'. Have you got a
                  ship?

ALI WHEY   Yes - the 'Ravishing Raisin.'.

OLD MAN   Good. Now listen, I want you to take off Sinbad
                  the Sailor - but don't get him mixed up with
                  Tinbad the Tailor - Sinbad's mother and the
                  Princess Yasmin. Got that?

ALI WHEY   Yes, Sinbad the Tailor -

BAK ALI   No, Tinbad the Sailor.

OLD MAN   No, the other way round.

BAK ALI   Sailor the Tinbad?

OLD MAN   No! No!

ALI WHEY   Tintor the Sailbad!

BAK ALI   And the Princess and her mother.

OLD MAN   His mother!

BAK ALI	His mother? Funny Princess.
OLD MAN	I'll write it down. But are you on?
ALI WHEY	Certainly. If it's nautical –
BAK ALI	and naughty –
ALI WHEY & BAK ALI	then we're on!

MUSIC 17   Nautical and Naughty

(Close traverse tabs and fly out frontcloth during number.)

ALL THREE
    Three
    Nautical types are we,
    Loitering by the sea,
Looking for fun,
Dastardly deeds to be done.

ALI WHEY & BAK ALI
    We're drips,
    Hanging about the ships,
    Looking for ocean trips.

OLD MAN
Hoping like mad
We'll have a chance to be bad.

ALI WHEY
We'll shiver all your timbers and we'll lead the
                      cat astray;

BAK ALI
We'll even box the compass in a pugilistic way.

ALL THREE
    We're males
    Waiting for icy gales
    In January sails –

OLD MAN
This is your chance
I'll book your trip in advance.

ALL THREE
It's fun to push the boat out when there's lots
                   of loot to share –
If it's nautical and naughty we'll be there.

(Dance.)

ALI WHEY
We'll weevil all your biscuits and we'll mutiny
                   the crew,

BAK ALI
And if you're running short of eggs we'll make
                 the ship lay 'two'.

ALL THREE
    We're crooks,

SINBAD THE SAILOR

Eager to cook the books,
Giving you nasty looks.

OLD MAN   Just for a meal,
We'd run away with the keel.

ALL THREE   We'll take the wind out of your sails and tamper
with your spare -
If it's nautical and naughty we'll be there!

BLACKOUT

(Open traverse tabs.)

I - 3 - 28   SCENE 3   Aboard the 'Sublime Sultana'

(Fullset. A large Arab Dhow running stem to
stern across the stage so one side of the vessel
faces us as a low backing about a foot in front of
the rostrum. In the C is a cabin with double
doors. Set inside is the galley with an oven at
the back - see 'Special Instructions' - There is
a shelf on one side of it on which is a large pie-
dish. A large kitchen table in front of the oven
on which is the following: a mixing bowl, sieve,
rolling pin, jug of water, packet of flour, packet
of salt and a slab of ready-made pastry.
The lights come up and SINBAD and CHORUS are
discovered on stage.)

MUSIC 18   A Very Good Ship

SINBAD   I've got a ship that's a very good ship
With a very good turn of speed.
Her great tall mast makes her very fast -
She's a very good ship indeed, indeed,
She's a very good ship indeed.

I've got a ship that's a very good ship
With a very good turn of speed.
She proudly rides on the strongest tides -

CHORUS   Her great tall mast makes her very fast -

SINBAD   She's a very good ship indeed, indeed,
She's a very good ship indeed.

I've got a ship that's a very good ship
    With a very good turn of speed.
Her wake gleams white in the dark of night -

CHORUS   Her great tall mast makes her very fast -
                She proudly rides on the strongest tides -

SINBAD   She's a very good ship indeed, indeed,
                    She's a very good ship indeed.

I've got a ship that's a very good ship
    With a very good turn of speed.
She's long and slim and her lines are trim -

CHORUS   Her great tall mast makes her very fast -
                She proudly rides on the strongest tides -
                Her wake gleams white in the dark of night -

SINBAD   She's a very good ship indeed, indeed,
                    She's a very good ship indeed.

I've got a ship that's a very good ship
    With a very good turn of speed.
She glides with ease on the lightest breeze -

CHORUS   Her great tall mast makes her very fast -
                She proudly rides on the strongest tides -
                Her wake gleams white in the dead of night -
                She's long and slim and her lines are trim -

SINBAD   She's a very good ship indeed, indeed,
                    She's a very good ship indeed -

CHORUS   A very good ship -

SINBAD   She's a very good ship -

CHORUS   A very good ship -

ALL   She's a very good ship indeed!

SINBAD   Time to stand down. You can go off watch till
                dinner time, lads.

CHORUS   Aye, aye, Captain. Thank you, Captain, etc.
                (they drift off L and R)

SINBAD   That reminds me. Mother wants Mr Tinbad to
                help her in the galley. I'd better find him.

TINBAD   (off) Drusila!

SINBAD   No need, he's found me.

TINBAD   (off) Not so fast, Drusila! Wait!

MUSIC 19   (Reprise 5 DRUSILA runs on L with a halter round her neck leading offstage. She stops and looks back then jerks her head. TINBAD comes flying on holding the other end of the halter and goes head over heels to DRUSILA's intense amusement.)

SINBAD   Are you all right, Mr Tinbad?

TINBAD   Oh yes, just taking Drusila for her early morning laugh - I mean, walk. She does love a good joke, doesn't she?

DRUSILA   (nods and laughs even more heartily)

SINBAD   No, not really.

DRUSILA   (stops laughing and looks at him enquiringly)

SINBAD   She only likes rotten jokes.

DRUSILA   (draws herself up and stumps huffily R, stopping three times to toss her head, each time more witheringly than the last)

SINBAD   Stop overacting, Drusila.

DRUSILA   (kicks up a contemptuous back leg and exits R)

SINBAD   Would you mind helping in the galley, Mr Tinbad? The ship's cook was asking for you.

TINBAD   Asking for me? Then of course! Anything to help little - little - I mean, to help a little. (to cover his embarrassment breaks into false laugh then stops abruptly with a cough)

SINBAD   Are you feeling all right, Mr Tinbad?

TINBAD   All right? I'm feeling splendid! Marvellous! Wonderful! I've been asked to help in the galley! Yippee! (dead pan) I mean, yes, quite all right.

SINBAD   Are you sure?

TINBAD   Quite sure, my son - er - that is, the sun. Lovely sunny day, isn't it?

SINBAD   Yes, and I should watch out for that sun, it's very strong.

TINBAD	Exactly what I keep telling your dear - ship's cook.
SINBAD	Hmm. Well, don't work too hard. Perhaps I'd better send some more help. Another couple of hands.
TINBAD	Oh, don't bother, I brought both of mine with me.
SINBAD	Naval hands, Mr Tinbad. Seamen. (exit R)
TINBAD	She asked for me! Actually asked for me! This is it. (sets his bowler at jaunty angle, smooths an invisible crease from his umbrella and moves to cabin doors) Ah, what will she say? (knocks on R door) What will she do?
	(MRS SINBAD opens R door knocking TINBAD in the face and pushing him back out of sight behind the open door.)
MRS SINBAD	Yes? Nobody there. (shuts door)
TINBAD	Not quite what I had in mind. Ah well. (about to knock on R door again suddenly stops) Ah! (moves in front of L door and knocks on R one)
MRS SINBAD	(off) Yes? (opens L door and again hits him) Still nobody!
	(She is about to shut the door when some muffled noises come from TINBAD and he waves a hand round the edge of the door.)
	Aaah!
	(TINBAD comes from behind the door holding his nose.)
	Mr Tinbad! What are you playing at?
TINBAD	Horry, hut hoo hi he hiv her hore.
MRS SINBAD	I beg your pardon?
TINBAD	(shaking head to clear it) I said, 'Sorry, but you hit me with the door.'
MRS SINBAD	Oh, I'm so sorry.
TINBAD	No, no, my fault. My nose shouldn't have got in the way. I've come to help you.

SINBAD THE SAILOR

MRS SINBAD   Oh good. (opens R door) It's such a lovely day —
              let's work outside. Give me a hand with the table.

TINBAD   (helping her out with it) Are you sure? With your
              delicate complexion. The sun's very strong, you
              know.

MRS SINBAD   Oh, I think it's shady enough here. Now, we're
              going to make a pie.

TINBAD   Ah. What sort of pie?

MRS SINBAD   (looks around cautiously) Well, where's Drusila?

TINBAD   (aghast) You don't mean - Drusila pie?

MRS SINBAD   Mr Tinbad! How could you think that? Our sup-
              plier of fresh milk on board - where would you
              be without your pint of gold hump each morning?
              No, I just don't want her to hear. This sort of
              pie's not good for her.

TINBAD   Oh, I see. Well, she's not here now.

MRS SINBAD   (moving R looking) We must make quite sure.
              (to audience) You can't see her, can you?
              (audience reaction) Right, then I'll tell you. It's a -

              (DRUSILA looks on R, cocking an ear at them.)

              (to audience) What's the matter? Drusila!

              (DRUSILA disappears.)

              You saw her? (audience reaction) You saw
              Drusila? (audience reaction) Well, I never.

TINBAD   In that case, let's go over there.

MRS SINBAD   Good idea. (as they cross L, to audience) Now
              you will keep an eye out for her, won't you?
              (audience reaction) Good. Are you ready, Mr
              Tinbad?

TINBAD   More than too much, Mrs Sinbad.

MRS SINBAD   Well then, it's a -

              (DRUSILA puts her head on L.)

              (to audience) What? You saw her again? The minx!

              (DRUSILA disappears.)

(to TINBAD) Come here in the middle and I'll whisper it to you.

(They move C.)

I'll whisper it very quietly, Mr Tinbad.

(Dummy microphone rises C or descends from flies, as convenient.)

MRS SINBAD   It's a - (whispers in his ear - EFFECT 1 MRS SINBAD's voice booming out -) POMEGRANATE PIE!

(TINBAD clutches his ear and DRUSILA's laugh is heard off stage. The microphone disappears.)

She's diddled us! The trouble is - well, you know what pomegranates are like, don't you?

TINBAD   Yes, those round sort of fruit full of pips.

MRS SINBAD   Exactly, and all those pips get loose inside her and start to rattle. We'll just have to see she doesn't get anywhere near them. Would you get them for me, Mr Tinbad? They're down in the hold.

TINBAD   Of course, delighted. (exit R)

MRS SINBAD   (checking table) Now, have I got everything else?

MUSIC 20   (Reprise 5   DRUSILA creeps on L stealthily with a long cloak draped over her. As the audience reacts MRS SINBAD looks up. DRUSILA turns round hastily to display the other side of the cloak, on which is written in large child-like letters 'SHH! I'M INVIZIBLE')

Drusila, you silly girl! Of course you're not invisible.

DRUSILA   (stamps in frustration)

MRS SINBAD   You've spelt it wrong, anyway. Invisible has two 'z's. But I'm afraid I'll have to tie you up for a bit.

(DRUSILA immediately runs off L and MRS SINBAD starts after her.)

Drusila, come here! Come here this instant! (off L) Drusila, where are you?

TINBAD

(entering R with a shallow box of pomegranates)
Here we are, lovely fresh pomegranates. Oh!

MRS SINBAD

(off L) Drusila!

TINBAD ·

Tut-tut. Wandering about in this strong sun. I
must go after her with my umbrella. I wonder
where she wants these?

(DRUSILA's foot pushes on a tray L, which has a
little sign sticking up on it - again in child-like
writing - 'HEAR'. A very obvious rope is attached
to it going off L.)

AH! Hmm, somebody can't spell 'here', should
be an 'e' on the end. (puts box down on tray and
goes off L) Mrs Sinbad!

(As soon as he has gone the tray is whisked off
stage and DRUSILA's laugh is heard.

MUSIC 21

Reprise 15 ALI WHEY's face appears US over
the ship's side. He looks cautiously round.)

ALI WHEY

(sotto voce) All clear. (climbs over into ship)
Come on.

BAK ALI

(off) Hold on. I haven't finished putting on my
pirate gear.

ALI WHEY

Well, hurry up.

BAK ALI

(head appearing over side of ship) Right, ready!
Here I am - (climbs over side and reveals his
costume - long silver coloured underpants on his
lower half) the famous pirate Long Johns Silver.
(holds one leg and hops about) Ah! Ali lad!
(very obviously pulls a string inside his jacket and
a scraggy-looking canary flips up on his shoulder.
Ventriloquising badly:) Pieces of seven! Pieces of
seven! Pieces of seven!

ALI WHEY

Eight, you fool. And it's supposed to be a parrot,
anyway.

BAK ALI

What? (to bird) You told me you'd played the
part before. (as bird) I lied! (to bird) Get lost!
(releases string and bird flops out of sight)

ALI WHEY

Stop mucking about and give me the bombs.

BAK ALI

Give you my combs? I can't, not in front of all

these people.

ALI WHEY	Not combs, bombs.

BAK ALI   Oh - bombs. (leans over the side and produces
                 a box of bombs similar to the pomegranates)
                 Here we are. What do we want bombs for, though?

ALI WHEY   I told you. We plant them round the ship then,
                 when we've got our three prisoners, we blow the
                 ship up with them.

BAK ALI   You mean - they're live?

ALI WHEY   Of course.

BAK ALI   Waaah! (flings box into air)

ALI WHEY   (catching it) Careful! (puts box down gingerly
                 where TINBAD put the pomegranates) We haven't
                 got the prisoners yet. But remember, as we
                 move about the ship, look inconspicuous (eyes
                 the silver long johns) - well, fairly inconspicuous,
                 and if anyone asks, you're one of the crew.

BAK ALI   Leave it to me. I've got all the naval lingo ready.
                 (hitches trousers sailor fashion and strides R)
                 Ahoy, shipmates! Avast for'ard! (strides C)
                 Avast amidships!

                 (As he strides L MRS SINBAD enters L sees the
                 box and bends down to pick it up.)

                 Avast behind!

MRS SINBAD   (straightening up) I beg your pardon?

BAK ALI   (slipping to the other side of ALI WHEY) Quite
                 right. Watch what you're saying, Ali.

TINBAD   (entering L) Ah, you've found the pomegranates.

BAK ALI   No, they're -

ALI WHEY   (clamping a hand over BAK ALI's mouth) Belt up!

TINBAD   Are you the two men the Captain said he'd send
                 to help?

BAK ALI   No, we're the p -

ALI WHEY   (again clamping hand) Quiet! (to others) Yes,

SINBAD THE SAILOR

                              that's us.

MRS SINBAD   (moving to behind table) Ah, then come along, we're going to make a pie.

BAK ALI   Oh, goody!

TINBAD   (picking up bombs and moving to table) A pomegranate pie.

BAK ALI   Waah! (dives under table)

MRS SINBAD   What's he doing under there?

ALI WHEY   Er - getting a little shade. It's very hot here.

MRS SINBAD   It'll be hotter still when we put the pie in the oven.

ALI WHEY   I think I'll join him. (is about to)

MRS SINBAD   No, no, come here, both of you. We've got to make the pastry. Put those down, Mr Tinbad.

                  (BAK ALI crawls out to L of MRS SINBAD. TINBAD puts the box down.)

                  (to BAK ALI) You can help me sift the flour.

                  (She gives him the packet of flour and he starts to pour it all into the sieve she holds over basin.)

                  (to ALI WHEY) You can stand by to put the water in.

                  (ALI WHEY picks up jug. MRS SINBAD gestures to or picks up salt packet.)

                  And, Mr Tinbad, would you oblige me with a pinch or two?

TINBAD   Would I? Oh - salt - I see. Of course. (putting salt in) Ah, this takes me back. I used to help my granny make pastry.

MRS SINBAD   Really?

TINBAD   Yes, she always used to say the higher you sift the flour the lighter the pastry.

MRS SINBAD   Well, I've never heard that before. Let's try it. (holds sieve higher) This high?

TINBAD   Oh, higher.

MRS SINBAD   (moves sieve up) This high?

TINBAD   Higher still.

                      (MRS SINBAD and BAK ALI climb on table.)

MRS SINBAD   How about here?

TINBAD   Splendid.

ALI WHEY   Are you ready for the water yet?

                      (MRS SINBAD turns to him taking sieve with her.
                      BAK ALI follows still pouring flour.)

MRS SINBAD   No, not quite, we have to - oh dear.

                      (The flour has gone all over ALI WHEY. He gives
                      a gigantic sneeze which causes MRS SINBAD to
                      jerk the sieve and also get flour on BAK ALI.)

                      Bless you. (turns and sees BAK ALI) Well, I
                      think that's enough flour.

                      (BAK ALI gets down from table.)

TINBAD   Wait a minute, now I come to think of it, perhaps
                      it was the higher the water.

MRS SINBAD   Oh. Well, while I'm up here. Give me the jug.

                      (ALI WHEY does so and MRS SINBAD starts to
                      pour it into the basin.)

TINBAD   Yes, definitely the water. (takes off bowler and
                      holds it upturned while turning away to mop brow)

MRS SINBAD   (turning so she is unknowingly pouring the water
                      into his bowler) Pity you didn't remember that
                      before, Mr Tinbad.

TINBAD   It must be the heat. I could do with a nice cool
                      something. (replaces bowler on head) Waaah!

MRS SINBAD   I'm afraid you got it! Perhaps we'd better use
                      some ready made pastry before we have any more
                      accidents. Clear this stuff away, dears.

                      (ALI WHEY, BAK ALI and TINBAD remove mixing
                      bowl, water jug, flour, salt and sieve to shelf.
                      MRS SINBAD picks up ready made pastry dough.)

                      It just needs rolling out. (doing so) Bring me
                      the pie dish.

                      (TINBAD brings pie dish from the shelf.)

SINBAD THE SAILOR

	Hmm, I think the pastry will be a bit too big.
TINBAD	I could take a tuck in it for you.
BAK ALI	Or we could just pull a bit off. Like this bit.
ALI WHEY	And this bit.
BAK ALI	And this.
ALI WHEY	And this.

(They keep pulling bits off, flinging them over their shoulders, ALI WHEY at MRS SINBAD and BAK ALI at TINBAD. MRS SINBAD takes up rolling pin and knocks the bits into the audience, likewise TINBAD with his umbrella - concealed pieces suitable for this.)

MRS SINBAD   That's enough! We shan't have any left for the pie; and look at all this mess. (takes pastry and uses it as a floor cloth) That's better. Now we'll finish off the pie.

TINBAD   (picking up box) Shall I tip the pomegranates in?

(ALI WHEY and BAK ALI start to edge away.)

MRS SINBAD   Yes, perhaps you should do that from a great height, too.

(TINBAD is about to climb on to table.)

ALI WHEY &
BAK ALI   NO!

MRS SINBAD   Why not?

ALI WHEY   Because - er - er - my granny! She said never pour bombs - poms - from a height.

MRS SINBAD   Oh, very well.

(She and TINBAD start placing them in pie dish.)

They seem a bit hard. I'll soften 'em up a bit. (raises rolling pin to do so)

ALI WHEY &
BAK ALI   NO!

MRS SINBAD   What's wrong now?

BAK ALI   My granny. She said never pound a pom.

MRS SINBAD	But I don't think they're ripe. I like my poms in prime condition.
ALI WHEY	Don't worry, they are.
MRS SINBAD	Well, if you say so. (covers dish with pastry) There, just put the lid on and –
TINBAD	Intc the oven?
MRS SINBAD	Into the oven.
	(TINBAD opens the oven door.)
ALI WHEY & BAK ALI	Into the oven! Waaah!
	(They both rush US to dive over the side. – EFFECT 2 – Two big splashes – MRS SINBAD puts pie in oven pushing it through false back and shuts the oven door.)
MRS SINBAD	Funny time to go swimming.
TINBAD	I expect it's the heat.
MRS SINBAD	Perhaps I should have made a bombe glacé.
	(– EFFECT 3 Loud explosion – Oven collapses in pieces. MRS SINBAD faints into TINBAD's arms. DRUSILA runs on L and starts to laugh and also to rattle. CHORUS run on L and R.)
CHORUS	What is it? What's the matter? What's happened?
SINBAD	(entering L) What was that explosion?
TINBAD	I don't know – the pomegranate pie – perhaps a pip exploded.
SINBAD	A pip!
DRUSILA	(gives burst of laughter and rattle)
SINBAD	Drusila!
DRUSILA	(subsides)
TINBAD	I think I'd better take Mrs Sinbad below to recover.
MRS SINBAD	(as they move off) What? Where am I? The pie! Where's the pie?
	(The charred remains of the pie fall from the flies.)
TINBAD	It's just descended from a great height.

MRS SINBAD	Ah, granny's recipe.
	(TINBAD escorts MRS SINBAD off R.)
SINBAD	You lads can clear all this away.
CHORUS	Aye, aye, Captain.
	(During the following they tidy up and carry off the table and remains of the pie, leaving the cabin doors closed. DRUSILA is unable to contain her laughter any more.)
SINBAD	Oh, Drusila, do stop laughing and rattling - rattling!
DRUSILA	(stops laughing abruptly and edges away)
SINBAD	(pointing an admonitory finger) Drusila!
DRUSILA	(shakes her head but rattles even more, gives up and runs off L still rattling)
YASMIN	(entering R) Hullo, I seem to have missed all the excitement. Did something awful happen?
SINBAD	Not really. Just the oven blew up.
YASMIN	Well, I think I might blow up soon. It's very frustrating.
SINBAD	What is?
YASMIN	Falling in love with the wrong person.
SINBAD	I hoped you'd fallen in love with the right person.
YASMIN	Oh, I have, but he's the wrong person to please my father. He's not rich enough.
SINBAD	Well, if we're both talking about the same person, he's working on that.
YASMIN	How? We'll be getting to India soon and -
SINBAD	India? Who said anything about India?
YASMIN	My father. You told him you'd take me -
SINBAD	- to meet your future husband - and I think I've done that. And your future husband - who happens to be the Captain of this ship, by the way - he's sailing to the Diamond Isle.
YASMIN	The Diamond Isle!

SINBAD	Yes, I told you he was working on getting rich. On the Diamond Isle is the fabulous Valley of Diamonds full of fabulous diamonds lying about just waiting to be picked up.
YASMIN	Yes, and a lot of fabulous birds called Great Rocs flying about just waiting to pick up the picker-uppers.
SINBAD	Picker-uppers?
YASMIN	Well, you know what I mean. That's if you don't meet the fabulous Blackbeard the Giant and his fabulous pigmy cannibals first.
SINBAD	If I do I promise I won't stay for a meal.
YASMIN	Sinbad, I'm serious. It's too dangerous.
SINBAD	Nothing's too dangerous for me - with you as the prize.

MUSIC 22   I Would Dare

I would dare ev'ry hurricane,
For there's nothing under heaven that I fear.

YASMIN	You can trust in your strong right arm - There's no battle you can't win when I'm near.
SINBAD	I'll stride the world with my head up high, I am seeking for fresh fields and pastures new. I'll walk with sword unsheathed among the strangers -
YASMIN	For men are the most menacing of dangers -
BOTH	But there can be no challenge in the world That I/you wouldn't dare, I/you wouldn't dare for you/me.
SINBAD	In my dreams I always hold your hand,
YASMIN	When you travel in a foreign land.
BOTH	Walk in any direction, Love's my/your shield and protection.
SINBAD	I would dare ev'ry hurricane, ... etc.
CHORUS 1	(off L) Pirate ship on the starboard bow!
SINBAD	Pirates!

SINBAD THE SAILOR

YASMIN   How exciting!

                      (- <u>EFFECT 4 Cannon boom</u> - A puff of smoke
                      comes on UL and a cannon ball thuds on to stage.)

SINBAD   Yasmin, get below!

YASMIN   Not on your life!

                      (The prow of the 'Ravishing Raisin' appears UL
                      and stops a few feet in.)

SINBAD   (drawing sword) All hands on deck! Stand by to
                      repel boarders!

                      (DRUSILA runs on R followed by MRS SINBAD.)

MRS SINBAD   Drusila! Come here! It's not safe!

                      (A section of the 'Raisin's' side has been let
                      down as a short gangplank on to the 'Sultana's'
                      side. In the gap thus formed ALI WHEY appears
                      closely followed by some CHORUS PIRATES. BAK
                      ALI reluctantly brings up the rear and remains
                      on the plank holding a large club.)

ALI WHEY   Come on, lads, there's the two we want! Grab
                      'em!

SINBAD   Never!

<u>MUSIC 23</u>   (<u>PIRATES' Entrance and Fight</u>   SINBAD's attempt
                      to save YASMIN and MRS SINBAD is hampered by
                      having to fight two people at once, ALI WHEY and
                      a CHORUS PIRATE. Other CHORUS PIRATES hustle
                      YASMIN on board their ship and manage to get
                      MRS SINBAD on to the gangplank but they have to
                      turn their attention to DRUSILA who is putting up
                      a four-footed defence of her mistress. They chase
                      DRUSILA offstage and return fighting CHORUS
                      SAILORS. Meanwhile SINBAD has disarmed the
                      CHORUS PIRATE and now has the advantage over
                      ALI WHEY.)

ALI WHEY   Bak, do something!

                      (BAK ALI raises his club above his head but MRS
                      SINBAD grabs it from behind him and hits him.
                      However, in falling, BAK ALI knocks SINBAD away
                      from ALI WHEY, then hastily crawls offstage. The
                      CHORUS PIRATE recovers his sword and attacks

SINBAD again, along with two other CHORUS
PIRATES who return,having forced the CHORUS
SAILORS offstage and presumably vanquished
them. ALI WHEY wrenches the club back from
MRS SINBAD just as her son is disarmed and held
at sword point. ALI WHEY knocks SINBAD out with
the club. CHORUS PIRATE is about to despatch
SINBAD.)

Leave him! Get that woman on board!

(The CHORUS PIRATES turn their attention to MRS
SINBAD who struggles with them. BAK ALI looks
on cautiously.)

BAK ALI	Have we won?
ALI WHEY	Yes.
BAK ALI	(striding on stage, waving his sword aggressively) Ha, we showed 'em! Nobody else for a fight, eh?
TINBAD	(running on R, umbrella held sword-like) Yes, me!
BAK ALI	(runs behind ALI WHEY) Your turn.
	(CHORUS PIRATES exit with MRS SINBAD, to ship.)
TINBAD	Stop! You've got Mrs Sinbad!
ALI WHEY	That's right.
TINBAD	Then you must take me too! (rushing on to PIRATES' ship) Mrs Sinbad! Never fear, Tinbad is here!
ALI WHEY	Hey, wait a minute! (does a double-take)
ALI WHEY & BAK ALI	Tinbad!
ALI WHEY	That's the one we wanted, isn't it?
BAK ALI	Er - yes. Or was it the other one?
ALI WHEY	He'll do. That's the lot then. Let's go.
	(They board their ship as DRUSILA runs on R.)
	Go away! Shoo! Haul up the gangplank!
	(BAK ALI does so.)
	We don't want any dromedaries on board.
	(Drum roll as DRUSILA crouches down for a

SINBAD THE SAILOR

	racing start and runs full pelt off L. - <u>EFFECT 5</u> <u>Loud thump off L</u> - the 'Raisin'shakes.)
BAK ALI	(looking off L) We've got a dromedary on board.
ALI WHEY	Oh well. Cast off and get under way!
<u>MUSIC 24</u>	(The 'Raisin' glides off L. Lights dim, green spot onto <u>OLD MAN OF THE SEA</u> as he stumps on L.)
OLD MAN	The fools! They've muck'd their kidnap bid. Oh, I could stamp! Oops, nearly did. But even so that bungling shower Have left young Sinbad in my power. The lad can't swim. So I shan't slip, I'll raise a storm to sink the ship! Come wind! And wave! And thunder boom! And send him to a wat'ry doom!
	(- <u>EFFECT 6 Storm</u> - cont. through to Scene 4)
	He can't escape! I've won! I've won!
	(Exit L laughing evilly. White flash R and PERI enters.)
PERI	Not when you leave the job half done.
	(Makes a magic pass at SINBAD who comes round, staggers to his feet and clutches his head.)
SINBAD	Ooh. What's happened? A storm! My ship!
PERI	Is going to take a downwards trip.
SINBAD	But I -
PERI	Can't swim. I know, don't worry. With this you will.(puts a chain round his neck) Now dive in, hurry!
SINBAD	I hope you're right.
PERI	I am, you'll see.
	(SINBAD jumps over the side of the ship.)
	And that, Old Man's one up to me!
	BLACKOUT
	(Close traverse tabs. Fly in frontcloth for Scene 4.)

SCENE 4 The Shores of the Diamond Isle

MUSIC 25

(Open tabs when ready during scene to reveal
frontcloth - gauze if possible - of an island shore.
Storm Music - EFFECT 6 continues - Green spot
on to OLD MAN OF THE SEA who hobbles on L.
Thunder effect where indicated *.)

OLD MAN

Aha! (*) Ooh! Ouch! Hurrah! (*) Ow!   Eee!
Ah, pleased to have me back, I see.
Yes, hiss and boo and rant and rate,
But you lot don't appreciate
Just how I suffer for my art,
'Cos I can't stop storms once they start,
And storms are chronic for me gout.
At least, though, it's put Sinbad out,
And that he's gone beyond recall
I'll check up on me crystal ball. (produces ball)
There's instant replay on this model. (looks)
What! (throws ball down furiously, it bounces off L)
        He's escaped, the silly noddle!
That perishing Peri's struck again
And all me suffering's been in vain.
Then for revenge I'm really rootin',
And I know how I'll put the boot in!

(Illustrates emphatically, unfortunately against the
proscenium arch, gives a loud cry of pain and
stumbles off L. The storm dies out and the lights
come up as SINBAD staggers on R, rather bedraggled.)

SINBAD

Whew! I made it. And I really could swim thanks
to this amulet. So this is the Diamond Isle. Not
that I care about diamonds now. It's just good to
be on dry land. I wish I knew where Yasmin was,
though. She must be miles away on that pirate ship –
and Mother. I wonder if I'll ever see them again.

MUSIC 26

MRS SINBAD's Entrance

MRS SINBAD

(entering R) Sinbad!

SINBAD

Mother! How did you get here?

MRS SINBAD

By umbrella.

SINBAD

By umbrella?

MRS SINBAD

Yes dear, Mr Tinbad's umbrella. Upside down –

like a boat, you see. I sat in it and he pushed me along.

SINBAD   But how did you escape from the pirate boat?

MRS SINBAD   We didn't. We fell off it in the storm – and it's very lucky we did. Those pirates were going to sell us into slavery.

SINBAD   What! Yasmin too?

MRS SINBAD   Yes, all of us, in Egypt.

SINBAD   Egypt?

MRS SINBAD   Yes, they decided to go there because they'd taken the wrong man and they said some old man or other would be cross with them.

SINBAD   Old man? Was it the Old Man of the Sea?

MRS SINBAD   That's right! He told them to take you, not Tinbad. But I'm ever so glad they didn't, dear.

SINBAD   Thank you, Mother.

MRS SINBAD   Well, you haven't got an umbrella. I don't know what's keeping Mr Tinbad. (calling) Mr Tinbad!

TINBAD   (off R) Coming, dear lady.

              (He enters R, crabwise, facing audience holding his umbrella opened out to cover his front.)

              Just had to put my clothes out to dry.   Sinbad!

SINBAD   Mr Tinbad, you saved my mother's life. Let me shake your hand.

TINBAD   I daren't! I might drop my umbrella. It's all I've got between me and – me.

MRS SINBAD   Ah, I see.

TINBAD   Oh, I do hope not.

SINBAD   Mr Tinbad, Mother, somehow we've got to get to Egypt and save Yasmin.

TINBAD   Tricky. I don't think my umbrella will carry more than one.

SINBAD   A raft! That's it! We'll build one. Let's see if we can find some driftwood by the shore. (exit R)

MRS SINBAD   Or perhaps another couple of umbrellas. They're very useful, aren't they, Mr Tinbad?

TINBAD   Oh, indispensable.

(They exit R. OLD MAN OF THE SEA enters L 'disguised' under an old brown cloak with a coil of rope.)

OLD MAN   No, turn it up. This time just sit
And watch my heavy acting bit.
'Alas! Alack! And woe is me!' (comes out of character) Where is the fellow? I'll start again -
'Alas! A-'

SINBAD   (off R) I'll go inland and try to find some logs.

OLD MAN   Aha!

(SINBAD enters R.)

'Alas! Alack! And woe is me! And come to that, misery me, as well. '

SINBAD   Hullo, old man, what's wrong?

OLD MAN   'Ah, rather ask me what is right. My wife and family are starving. Our only hope was for my little son and I to gather diamonds in the Valley. Many weary miles we travelled to get here and now my boy is stricken with fever. Verily we are doomed! Doomed! ' (aside) Not bad this script, is it? (to SINBAD) 'If only someone would help me, one half of the gathering would be his; enough to buy a palace - a harem - a fleet of ships - a ..... '

SINBAD   Hold on. Ships did you say?

OLD MAN   Yes, there are many ships in the port nearby.'

SINBAD   Then I'll help you.

OLD MAN   'Noble youth!'

SINBAD   But how can I protect myself from the Giant and his pigmy cannibals?

OLD MAN   'Cannibals? Mere heresay.'

SINBAD   Really? And the birds, the Great Rocs?

OLD MAN   'Harmless.'

SINBAD | Then there's nothing to worry about. I'll just tell my mother and a friend what I'm doing.

OLD MAN | 'No, no, let me have the honour to inform the mother of such a peerless young fellow. (giving SINBAD rope) Take this and follow the path there to the mountain top. You can secure the rope firmly while you await me.'

SINBAD | All right. Well, here's a bit of luck! (exit L)

OLD MAN | Yes, luck indeed, but luck for me,

(MRS SINBAD and TINBAD -now fully clothed - start to enter R.)

The clever Old Man of the Sea!

(MRS SINBAD stops them in their tracks and they retreat offstage, putting their heads on to listen.)

MUSIC 27 (under speech) | Those cannibals mere hearsay? No!
Their appetites on him will grow.
The Rocs quite harmless? Not one whit!
For them he'll make a tasty bit.
So, young Sinbad, twixt one or t'other,
There's naught but bad news for your mother!

(Exit L, laughing evilly. MRS SINBAD and TINBAD emerge R.)

MRS SINBAD | The old whatsit!

TINBAD | Yes, if he'd been within umbrella's length I'd have poked him in the eye.

MRS SINBAD | Oh, Mr Tinbad, you're so brave!

TINBAD | Only because I - I - but there's no time for that now. We must save your son! Come, to the Valley of Diamonds!

MRS SINBAD | The Valley of Diamonds!

(They hasten L, then TINBAD suddenly doubles back.)

It's this way. Where are you going?

TINBAD | I forgot my umbrella.

(He retrieves it and as they exit L dim lights and bleed through gauze to Scene 5*.)

(* If a gauze is not used – BLACKOUT fly cloth
and fade up lights on Scene 5.)

SCENE 5   The Valley of Diamonds

MUSIC 28

(Diamond Ballet Fullset. A craggy mountain
scene, with glittering heaps of diamonds strewn
about the ground some of which come to life for
the ballet. UC a rock piece set on swivel, the
reverse side of which represents a huge bird.
Ballet finishes, diamonds subside or go offstage.)

SINBAD

(off) Nearly there! Gosh what a sight! Right,
made it!

(SINBAD enters L holding the end of a rope – rope
has been fitted over a pulley on the free end of an
arm pivoting on from behind the top of the L wing.)

OLD MAN

(off above) Good!

SINBAD

(rubbing arms) That was a long way to hang on,
but it's going to be worth it.

OLD MAN

(off) Can you see any diamonds?

SINBAD

Heaps and heaps of them. (leaves rope hanging
and starts to fill a sack from his belt) I'll soon
get a sackful.

OLD MAN

(off) Have you let go of the rope?

SINBAD

Yes.

OLD MAN

(off) Splendid!

SINBAD

I'll shout when I'm ready to come up.

OLD MAN

(off) Aye, shout away, shout loud and clear,
Shout all you want, for none will hear!

(He starts to laugh fiendishly and the rope slowly
begins to rise.)

SINBAD

What? Wait! The rope! (runs back and jumps up
trying to catch it) Don't take the rope!

OLD MAN

(off) I'll take both it and all your hope!

(Rope disappears.)

SINBAD

No, no, wait! I don't understand,
You ask'd me for –

OLD MAN   A helping hand?
A trick to lure you to your grave,
For it's not diamonds that I crave,
Revenge is all that's dear to me,
Since I'm the Old Man of the Sea!

(He gives a burst of mocking laughter - EFFECT 7
Laughter echoing and dying away to silence -)

SINBAD   He can't mean it. He can't! I must get out! I'll
climb out somehow - (runs to one side) Here!
(runs to other side) or here! (runs UC) or -
no good, the rocks are too smooth. Then help, I
must get help - Help! Help! HELP!

(- EFFECT 8 Echo of SINBAD's voice -)

There - I heard someone. HELP!

(- EFFECT 9 Echo reverberating round hilltops -)

I heard myself. I'm panicking. I must think.
There must be some way to escape. The Old Man
of the Sea may think he's had his revenge but
this isn't my grave - yet. I'll explore along here.

(Exit SINBAD R. A brief pause then two prolonged
shrieks are heard growing in volume and suddenly
MRS SINBAD and TINBAD jump on L from as high as
possible, clutching TINBAD's umbrella as a para-
chute to land in a muddled heap. TINBAD carries
coil of rope.)

TINBAD   Are you all right, Mrs Sinbad? Not quite a three
point landing, I'm afraid.

MRS SINBAD   (rising, rubbing behind) Never mind, it was quite
enough for me on one point.

SINBAD   (running on R) Whatever was - Mother! Mr Tinbad!
How did you get here?

MRS SINBAD &
TINBAD   By umbrella!

MRS SINBAD   It's the only way to travel, dear. We've come to
rescue you because that wicked old man told you a
lot of fibs.

TINBAD   Yes, Blackbeard and his pigmies are cannibals.

MRS SINBAD	And the Great Rocs aren't exactly vegetarians, either. So we've come to get you out of here.
SINBAD	Good! But how?
MRS SINBAD	Ah, we've thought of that. But before we go tell me, are these great big shiny things really diamonds?
SINBAD	Of course, but never mind that –
TINBAD	They are rather large, aren't they? Rather vulgar really.
MRS SINBAD	Um, very vulgar. Still, as we're here, we might as well take a few.
TINBAD	Just one or two perhaps.
MRS SINBAD	Only as souvenirs, of course.
TINBAD	Of course.
MRS SINBAD	Have a sack!
	(She produces two sacks and TINBAD and MRS SINBAD start filling them as hard as they can go.)
SINBAD	Mother, we must –
MRS SINBAD	Yes, shan't be a jiffy, dear. I'm just thinking about that fifty sequins rent I owe. (picks up an exceptionally large diamond) Would this cover it?
SINBAD	Cover it? It would smother it. That must be worth at least a million sequins.
MRS SINBAD	A million? (nervelessly her fingers let the gem drop on her toes) Ow!
TINBAD	Oh, Mrs Sinbad.
MRS SINBAD	Don't worry. At that price the agony's delicious. (puts it in her sack) There, that'll do, I think. Well, perhaps just another million for a rainy day. (puts another gem into sack)
TINBAD	Well, now you mention it, Mrs Sinbad, the weather forecast's not too good.
MRS SINBAD	Really?
TINBAD	Really.

SINBAD THE SAILOR

(They stuff more diamonds into their sacks.)

SINBAD   Mother! Mr Tinbad! What's the use of diamonds if we can't get out of here?

MRS SINBAD   I told you, dear, we thought of that.

TINBAD   Yes, we brought a rope. Look.

MRS SINBAD   So all we have to do is climb up it.

SINBAD   How? By the Indian Rope Trick?

MRS SINBAD   Don't be silly, dear. One end's fastened to the top and -

SINBAD   Which end?

TINBAD   Oh, the other end. The rope's got two ends, you see. This end -

MRS SINBAD   And this end -

TINBAD &   Oh. We made a boo-boo.
MRS SINBAD

SINBAD   Oh well, it was a nice thought. But what happens now?

MUSIC 29   (BLACKBEARD Music - EFFECT 10 Thunderous footsteps -)

                    What's that?

MRS SINBAD   Roadworks perhaps?

TINBAD   No, it's getting nearer......

SINBAD   And nearer .....

MRS SINBAD   It's -

ALL THREE   Blackbeard the Giant!

                    (BLACKBEARD enters L. He should look as large and as terrifying as possible with built-up boots, a high frizzy wig and a bushy black beard.)

BLACKBEARD   AHA!

ALL THREE   Run!

                    (They run R and are met by the PIGMIES - CHORUS CHILDREN - who leap on flourishing spears and uttering bloodthirsty cries. The three stop in C.)

BLACKBEARD   Look what's dropped in - din-dins!

                    (PIGMIES jump up and down with squeals of
                    excitement.)

                    Which one shall we have? This one? (prods MRS
                    SINBAD)

PIGMIES   Yum!

MRS SINBAD   No, I'm too old and tough.

TINBAD   Nonsense!

MRS SINBAD   Shut up, Mr Tinbad! I am!

BLACKBEARD   Or this one? (prods TINBAD)

PIGMIES   Yum-yum!

TINBAD   No, no! I'm not worth even one yum let alone two.

BLACKBEARD   Or this one? (prods SINBAD)

PIGMIES   Yum-yum-yum!

SINBAD   All right, take me, but leave them.

BLACKBEARD   Ah, big-hearted, eh? But not very big otherwise.
                    And I have to think of my little Pigmies. They
                    won't grow if I don't feed 'em, will they? (laughs
                    uproariously) So I think - we'll have you all!

MUSIC 30   (PIGMIES go into paroxysms of delighted squeals.
                    Feasting Dance During which the three are tied
                    together with TINBAD's rope. MRS SINBAD is in
                    the middle facing DS with SINBAD facing R and
                    TINBAD facing L on either side of her. Just as
                    the three victims are about to be impaled on the
                    PIGMIES' spears dim lights - EFFECT 11 Flapping
                    wings and croaking - All freeze then look up. A
                    cut out of bird flies across sky - see 'Special
                    Instructions' - from L to R. PIGMIES squeal in
                    terror.)

                    A roc! A roc!

PIGMIES   Ugh! Ugh!

                    (PIGMIES flee off L and BLACKBEARD hurries after
                    them.)

BLACKBEARD   Wait for me, you little perishers! Wait for me!

SINBAD THE SAILOR

                   (As he disappears off L a larger bird cut-out
                   flies across sky from R to L.)

TINBAD   It's getting closer!

SINBAD   It's blotting out the sun!

MRS SINBAD   What can we do?

SINBAD &
TINBAD   Run!

                   (Lights fade as all three start to run, but as each
                   is facing a different direction they get nowhere.)

ALL THREE   Too late!

                   (End fade in BLACKOUT. Swivel rock piece to
                   reveal bird - if the facilities are available of
                   course the Roc can be flown in in vision - There
                   is a white flash R, lights up and PERI is on stage R.)

PERI   No, just in time. I brought the Roc.
                   Stand by - you're going to feel a shock.

                   (PERI makes a magic pass at them. MUSIC TINGLE
                   to which they react and the rope drops away - the
                   ends have been held by SINBAD and TINBAD in their
                   US hands.)

ALL THREE   We're free!

PERI   And free to fly away.

ALL THREE   To fly?

PERI   Yes, on the Roc.

SINBAD   I say!
                   What an adventure! Come on, Mum!

MRS SINBAD   I'm feeling queasy in me tum.

TINBAD   No need to worry, I'll be there. (lifts sack)
                   Can we take luggage in the air?

PERI   Why, yes. But mount.

                   (They do. If the Roc is to be flown out in vision,
                   but it is impossible to lift the three principals as
                   well, they must run behind the Roc as if to mount it
                   there and in reality conceal themselves behind the
                   rock piece. If using Roc/rock piece see opposite.)

Now fly these three
To Egypt far across the sea!

(BLACKOUT   Swivel piece to rock side. SINBAD,
MRS SINBAD and TINBAD conceal themselves behind it. Lights up - PERI is R on rostrum, OLD
MAN OF THE SEA has entered DL and is shaking a
fist at her as a cut-out of the Roc with three figures
on it crosses from L to R at the top of the sky.
- EFFECT 12 Roc croaking and flapping wings fades -
away - Flying Music)

MUSIC 31

CURTAIN

MUSIC 32   Entracte

PART 2 SCENE 1   The Slave Market at Cairo

Fullset. A crowded Eastern market scene. A dais C in front of the
rostrum, which is the SLAVE MASTER's stand, on it is a notice :-
'GRAND SLAVE AUCTION TODAY AT NOON'. R a gateway labelled
'SLAVE PEN'. L a shop piece, 'SEED MERCHANT', with a large sack
outside it inscribed 'BIRD SEED'.

As the curtains open the SLAVE MASTER is discovered flourishing a
whip, with CHORUS GIRLS being brought as prospective SLAVES by
the CHORUS MEN for sale to the SLAVE MASTER.

MUSIC 33   Slaves

SLAVE MASTER   Slaves of ev'ry race and hue,
         You can try them here,
         You can buy them here.
    There must be a slave for you;
         They are here today,
         They are on display.
    Sloe-eyed beauties from the orient;
    Slaves of copper-coloured silk;
    From the coldness of the north-lands,
    Blue-eyed slaves with skins of milk -
         All these wonders that I tell you,
         Here today I come to sell you.

(CHORUS MEN encourage SLAVES to dance to
demonstrate their qualities.)

All the latest shapes and sizes,
         Subtle shades of hair and eye,
You can take them as your prizes,
         Anyone who cares to buy.
Rarer jewels than words can tell you
Are the beauties that I sell you -
         Slaves!

(The SLAVES are herded off R to 'SLAVE PEN' and
CHORUS MEN disperse off L.)

ALI WHEY   (off L) Drusila, come here!

MUSIC 34   (DRUSILA's Entrance - runs on L with ALI WHEY holding on to the other end of the halter.)

BAK ALI	(off L) Yasmin, come here!
	(YASMIN runs on L also on a halter, which BAK ALI is holding on to.)
ALI WHEY	(to DRUSILA) Now, sit.
DRUSILA	(refuses firmly)
BAK ALI	(to YASMIN) Well, you sit.
YASMIN	Don't you tell me to sit!
BAK ALI	(slips to other side of ALI WHEY) I didn't. He did.
ALI WHEY	Yes, he did.
BAK ALI	(to ALI WHEY) Now you've got me confused.
YASMIN	You're always confused. Both of you. Aren't they, Drusila?
DRUSILA	(nods)
YASMIN	You're completely incompetent! Aren't they, Drusila?
DRUSILA	(nods)
YASMIN	In fact, you're a couple of silly, stupid, bone-headed, idiotic, clod-hopping, witless, footling, half-baked, brainless boobies! Aren't they, Drusila?
DRUSILA	(looks at her in astonishment for a moment then nods rapidly several times)
BAK ALI	You missed one.
DRUSILA	(gives another nod)
BAK ALI	That's better.
	(Enter SLAVE MASTER R.)
YASMIN	And how dare you think of selling me as a slave!
SLAVE MASTER	What was that?
	(He cracks his whip, which startles DRUSILA, ALI WHEY and BAK ALI and they run behind YASMIN.)
	I said, 'what was that?' (cracks whip again)

BAK ALI	It was you cracking your whip.
SLAVE MASTER	No, what was that about a slave? I'm the Slave Master here. (cracks whip)
BAK ALI	I think he's developing a nasty habit.
YASMIN	Well, if you're thinking of buying me you can think again.
SLAVE MASTER	Ah, one of the fiery ones, eh? Good. I like a bit of spirit. How much?
ALI WHEY	Well, we were thinking of -
SLAVE MASTER	Too much.
ALI WHEY	Oh. Then how about - ?
SLAVE MASTER	Still too much.
BAK ALI	It needs a business man to handle this. Leave it to me. (moves to SLAVE MASTER) Now look here, my good fellow -
	(SLAVE MASTER cracks whip. BAK ALI runs behind ALI WHEY.)
	I agree. Much too much. Name your own price.
YASMIN	Can't you even fix a price for me? Well, I will! Twenty thousand sequins!
SLAVE MASTER	Fifteen.
BAK ALI	Ten!
ALI WHEY	Shut up!
BAK ALI	Sorry. I meant five.
SLAVE MASTER	Well -
BAK ALI	We'll throw in Drusila as well.
DRUSILA	(draws herself up and stalks off L)
BAK ALI	In that case - four.
SLAVE MASTER	Done. Here you are, three thousand sequins. (hands over a purse)
ALI WHEY	Three? You just said -
	(SLAVE MASTER cracks his whip.)

BAK ALI	Two. Here's a thousand change.
SLAVE MASTER	Thank you.
YASMIN	Oh, you - you - !
SLAVE MASTER	Save it. my little beauty. Good day, gentlemen, a pleasure to do business with you.
BAK ALI	And with you.
	(SLAVE MASTER exits with YASMIN into pen, locking it behind him.)
ALI WHEY	A fine business man you turned out to be.
BAK ALI	I know. I've got a flair for it.
	(Sky begins to darken. - EFFECT 13 Roc's flapping wings approaching - CHORUS and CHILDREN run across the stage looking skywards.)
CHORUS & CHILDREN	The Roc! The Roc!
BAK ALI	(looking offstage after them) What's the matter with them?
ALI WHEY	They don't like modern music.
BAK ALI	Fuddie-duddies. Er - one o'clock, two o'clock, three o'clock rock -
ALI WHEY	Yeah! Four o'clock, five o'clock, six o'clock -
	(- EFFECT 14 Loud Roc croaking -)
BAK ALI	Funny backing group.
MUSIC 35	(Flying Music Cut-out Roc crosses from R to L on cyc. They look up and see it.)
ALI WHEY & BAK ALI	WAAH!
ALI WHEY	It's landing! Hide!
	(ALI WHEY runs behind dais, BAK ALI runs behind bird seed sack.)
	Not there!
BAK ALI	Why not? (looks at front of sack) Aaah!
	(He runs and joins ALI WHEY behind dais and they

peer over the top of it.)

ALI WHEY	(pointing upwards off L and whispering) It's up there.
BAK ALI	Ooh, yes, and there's people getting off it.
ALI WHEY	It's Sinbad and the two we kidnapped. Get down!

(They disappear behind the dais.)

SINBAD	(off L) Thank you, Roc.

(- EFFECT 15 Roc croaking once and wings flapping away - SINBAD enters L)

Come on!

MRS SINBAD	(off L) Coming, dear. (enters L) So this is Cairo. Seems a bit deserted. Must be early closing day.
SINBAD	Where's Mr Tinbad?
TINBAD	(entering L with sacks of diamonds) Here! Just bringing the in-flight bags.
MRS SINBAD	Oh yes, we don't want to forget our little bits of duty-free. We might need them to rescue Yasmin.
SINBAD	Look! There's going to be a Slave Auction; and Yasmin might be in that Slave Pen even now. If I could just get in there -

(As he tries to force the gate the SLAVE MASTER enters R and cracks whip, which so startles TIN-BAD that he leaps into MRS SINBAD's arms.)

SLAVE MASTER	Stand back!

(BAK ALI stands up.)

ALI WHEY	(pulling him down) Not you!
SLAVE MASTER	What do you want?
SINBAD	Oh - er - well -
TINBAD	(getting down) So sorry, Mrs Sinbad -
MRS SINBAD	Never mind, if there's a next time -

(SLAVE MASTER cracks whip again and MRS SINBAD leaps into TINBAD's arms and he collapses.)

MRS SINBAD	Will you be doing that again?
SLAVE MASTER	I might.
MRS SINBAD	Than we'll stay down here.
SLAVE MASTER	(to SINBAD) Well? What do you want?
SINBAD	I want to find a slave.
SLAVE MASTER	Then you're talking to the right man. I'm the Slave Master. Any particular kind of slave?
SINBAD	Oh, yes - very particular.
SLAVE MASTER	Come with me then. I'll show you the goods for sale. (unlocks slave pen and exits into it)
SINBAD	Thanks. (to others) I'll see what I can find out.
	(SINBAD exits R. TINBAD rises and helps MRS SINBAD up.)
TINBAD	I hope you didn't hurt yourself.
MRS SINBAD	Oh, never mind about me. It's Yasmin I'm worried about. We'd better get those changed for some money in case she's in that auction - or do you think old Whipcrack will take diamonds?
ALI WHEY	(bobbing up and down) Diamonds?
MRS SINBAD	Yes, diamonds.
BAK ALI	(bobbing up and down) Diamonds?
MRS SINBAD	Are you all right, Mr Tinbad?
TINBAD	I was about to say, no.
MRS SINBAD	You're not all right?
TINBAD	Oh no. I mean, yes.
MRS SINBAD	Yes - well, that's cleared that up.
TINBAD	Yes, I'm all right, but no, I don't think he'll take diamonds.
MRS SINBAD	Well, they are rather big diamonds.
ALI WHEY	(bobbing up and down) Big diamonds?
MRS SINBAD	Well, you know they - are you sure you're all right?

SINBAD THE SAILOR

TINBAD   Never better. Why?

MRS SINBAD   You keep repeating everything I say.

TINBAD   Ah, I think there's a funny sort of echo here.

MRS SINBAD   A funny sort of echo?

ALI WHEY   (bobbing up and down) That's it, an echo!

TINBAD   There! Now if I say 'Hullo' –

ALI WHEY   (off) Hullo!

TINBAD   You see, it says hullo back.

BAK ALI   (bobbing up) Hullo, Tinbad.

ALI WHEY   (pulling him down) You fool!

MRS SINBAD   Now that is a funny sort of echo. Insulting too.
                  Let's find a nicer one.

                  (MRS SINBAD and TINBAD exit L with sacks. ALI
                  WHEY and BAK ALI emerge from behind dais.)

ALI WHEY   Diamonds!

BAK ALI   Two sacks of them!

ALI WHEY   And they're going to cash them in –

BAK ALI   They'll get a fortune! There's only one thing to do.

ALI WHEY   What?

                  (CHILDREN enter in single file.)

BAK ALI   Steal it! (sees CHILDREN) Ali, watch what
                  you're saying in front of these innocent little
                  darlings.

CHILD 1   We're not darlings!

CHILD 2   And we're not innocent.

CHILD 3   We're all in N.A.P.P.Y.

BAK ALI   Really? I'd have thought you were past that stage.

CHILD 4   Not nappies! The N.A.P.P.Y.

BAK ALI   What, just the one between you?

CHILD 5   No, the (spells it out) N – A – P – P – Y.

BAK ALI   Oh, that Nappy. Why didn't you say so.

SINBAD THE SAILOR

(to ALI WHEY) What are they talking about?

(ALI WHEY shrugs.)

CHILD 6 The National Association of Purloining Pilfering Youth.

BAK ALI Then, my little dears, this is a lucky day for you. You see before you two of the finest purloiners and pilferers in the business. And what's more we're thieves as well. Shall we demonstrate?

ALI WHEY Let's.

MUSIC 36 The Professionals

ALI WHEY & BAK ALI Watch out! We're the professionals; Our concern is hanky-panky.

ALI WHEY Watch out! (takes BAK ALI's watch) Obviously You must steal a watch that goes.

BAK ALI It's gone!

(CHILD 1 steals watch from ALI WHEY.)

ALI WHEY & BAK ALI You would never believe it That if we want to steal a hanky

BAK ALI Here's the way that we thieve it

(ALI WHEY produces a handkerchief prepares to sneeze.)

From underneath your nose. (takes handkerchief)

ALI WHEY At-CHOO! (sneezes into his hands)

(CHILD 2 steals handkerchief from BAK ALI.)

CHILDREN We are born predators and we never knew we knew it. We would like to steal the show, is this the way we do it?

ALI WHEY If our drift you have took

BAK ALI If you've got the wit and impetus,

ALI WHEY & BAK ALI Then you'll go down in the book As professionals like us.

(dance)

CHILDREN After all your good advice we're getting the ide-ar,

We will go and try and steal the froth from
                        Grandma's be-are!

ALI WHEY &   Be an 'A' level sneak!
BAK ALI   You can be bad or even wus,

(CHILD 3 and 4 respectively steal ALI WHEY and
BAK ALI's jackets - made with velcro seams.)

If you acquire the technique
      Of professionals like us!

(CHILD 5 and 6 remove ALI WHEY and BAK ALI's
trousers - also made with velcro - CHILDREN run
off L. ALI WHEY and BAK ALI suddenly realise
they are down to their underwear and chase off
after them.
CHORUS MEN start to assemble for the Slave
Auction. SINBAD enters R. MRS SINBAD and
TINBAD enter L with a carrier bag.)

SINBAD   Mother, Mr Tinbad! I've seen her!

TINBAD   Is she going to be in the sale?

SINBAD   In it? She's going to be the sale. The Slave
              Master's sure he'll get a better price for her
              that way.

MRS SINBAD   Oh, good. Well, we don't want to get her on the
              cheap, do we?

SINBAD   But suppose somebody outbids us.

TINBAD   I don't think they'll be able to.

MRS SINBAD   No, dear, we've just cashed in the diamonds -
              and look!

(She brings a large purse from carrier as ALI
WHEY and BAK ALI look on surreptitiously L.)

Do you know how much is in there?

SINBAD   No, how much?

MRS SINBAD   A million sequins! And we've got another eleven
              just like it.

(ALI WHEY and BAK ALI exchange delighted looks
and disappear.)

SINBAD   Twelve million sequins in a carrier bag!

MRS SINBAD   Yes, but it's all right he didn't charge extra for it.

TINBAD   When does the sale start?

SINBAD   He said on the crack of noon.

                  (A whip cracks off R.)

TINBAD   Noon's cracked.

                  (There's a buzz of excitement as SLAVE MASTER
                  enters R with YASMIN and they mount the dais.)

SLAVE MASTER   Ladies and gentlemen! It's a very special sale
                  today. I've got just one lot for you, but what a
                  lot I've got.

MRS SINBAD   What's he think he's selling? Smarties?

SLAVE MASTER   (cracks whip) This is no joking matter. Just look
                  at this slave. Beautiful body work. And with lines
                  like that you get a very economical food consump-
                  tion. Guaranteed entirely unused, no previous
                  owner –

YASMIN   Oh, get on with it, man, and just sell me!

                  (CROWD laughs.)

SLAVE MASTER   As you can see, a very lively model. So, who'll
                  open the bidding for me at say – twenty thousand
                  sequins?

SINBAD   I will!

SLAVE MASTER   Thank you, sir. Twenty thousand I'm bid.

CHORUS 1   Twenty five.

CHORUS 2   Thirty!

CHORUS 1   Thirty five!

SINBAD   Fifty!

MRS SINBAD   Sixty!

TINBAD   Seventy!

MRS SINBAD   Eighty!

TINBAD   Let's not be mean – a hundred thousand!

                  (Bidding continues during following speeches.)

SINBAD THE SAILOR

SINBAD   Mr Tinbad! Mother! We mustn't bid against
                  each other.

MRS SINBAD   Sorry, dear.

TINBAD   We got carried away.

SLAVE MASTER   A hundred and fifty thousand I'm bid. Any
                  advance?

                  (SINBAD is about to bid again as a STRANGER
                  enters DR and indicates a bid by a slight gesture.)

                  Two hundred thousand on my right!

SINBAD   Three!

                  (STRANGER gestures.)

SLAVE MASTER   Four.

SINBAD   Five!

                  (STRANGER gestures. At the same time ALI WHEY
                  and BAK ALI creep on L behind MRS SINBAD. ALI
                  WHEY carries a bag labelled 'LOOT' and BAK ALI
                  a pair of scissors. ALI WHEY holds 'LOOT' bag
                  beneath MRS SINBAD's carrier - in her DS hand -
                  while BAK ALI cuts across it with the scissors, so
                  that the lower half of the carrier with the purses
                  of money in it falls into the 'LOOT' bag. ALI WHEY
                  and BAK ALI then creep offstage again.)

SLAVE MASTER   Six.

SINBAD   Seven!

                  (STRANGER gestures.)

SLAVE MASTER   Eight.

SINBAD   Nine!

                  (SLAVE MASTER looks towards STRANGER expec-
                  tantly, but he hesitates.)

SLAVE MASTER   Nine -

                  (STRANGER makes a slightly different gesture.)

                  and fifty?

                  (STRANGER nods.)

Nine hundred and fifty thousand then –

SINBAD   A million!

SLAVE MASTER   One million! (looks expectantly at STRANGER)
One million against you, sir.

(STRANGER shakes his head.)

(looking round generally) All done? (cracks whip)
Sold to the gentleman on my left at a million sequins!

MRS SINBAD   Huh, chicken feed!

SLAVE MASTER   Your slave, sir –

(YASMIN flies to SINBAD.)

SINBAD   Yasmin!   } together

YASMIN   Sinbad!

SLAVE MASTER   (putting out hand) And my money, sir.

SINBAD   Mother, the money.

MRS SINBAD   (putting hand in carrier) Yes, here you – (finds
her hand waggling in space) Aaah! I've been
robbed!

(General buzz of excitement.)

SLAVE MASTER   No money, then no slave.

(Wrenches YASMIN away.)

And don't waste my time again! (cracks whip)

SINBAD   Yasmin!

(The STRANGER intercepts SLAVE MASTER as he is
dragging a protesting YASMIN away. There is a
brief whispered consultation between them which
TINBAD notices and he edges over to try and overhear. The consultation ends with nodding agree-
ment from the SLAVE MASTER and the STRANGER
hurries off DR. Meanwhile the CHORUS have turned
on SINBAD and MRS SINBAD in derision, accusing
them of never having had any money etc. before
they drift off L and R. SLAVE MASTER drags YASMIN
into the pen.)

What are we going to do?

TINBAD

Don't worry. I've got a lead. That man who was bidding against you was arranging something and I intend to find out what. (hurries DR)

MRS SINBAD

Be careful, Mr Tinbad.

TINBAD

For you, of course. But then I always am. (turns and trips over umbrella) Well, almost always. (exits DR)

SINBAD

Oh, Mother.

MRS SINBAD

I know, dear, but - well, life's like that. Just when you're on top of the world the bottom falls out of everything - like my carrier bag. But when that happens, dear, all you need is a new bottom. Perhaps I could have put that better.

SINBAD

(laughs) Oh, Mother! I do love you. You're so silly!

MRS SINBAD

I know, dear. But that's what mothers are for, to be silly - at the right moment.

MUSIC 37

Come to Mother

When you're just a tiny tot
And your finger hurts a lot,
        Come to Mother.
When you first appear at school
And your friends say you're a fool,
        Come to Mother.
In the busy time of growing, when you don't know
                                who you are,
And each day or two you hitch your wagon to a
                                diff'rent star,
There's comfort round the corner, and it isn't
                                very far -
........Come to Mother.

SINBAD

Though it nearly makes you cry
When you don't see eye to eye,

MRS SINBAD

        Come to Mother.

SINBAD

Though you sometimes have a row,
And you think that she's a nuisance,

MRS SINBAD

        Come to Mother.

SINBAD	When the world is hard and callous and the future's far from bright,
MRS SINBAD	And you feel that you have not the strength to carry on the fight,
BOTH	You'll know that there's one place to go where ev'rything's all right - ....Come to Mother.

(SINBAD and MRS SINBAD exit arm in arm, as
they go lights fade to BLACKOUT.
Open traverse tabs.)

SCENE 2 Khul Dissac in Cairo   II - 2 - 69

(Frontcloth. Eastern street scene. There is a
finger sign on it LC 'TO THE DESERT', pointing L.
Set diagonally across L exit is a wall, on which is
a sign 'KHUL DISSAC'.

MUSIC 38

Following Music STRANGER enters R closely followed by TINBAD - copying the STRANGER's every
step with elaborate stealth. The STRANGER is
obviously trying to find his way somewhere. He
stops to look at the finger sign and hurries L only
to meet the wall, which puzzles him. He shrugs
and turns, TINBAD immediately pretends to be
interested in the contents of a shop window. ALI
WHEY and BAK ALI enter R, ALI WHEY carrying
the loot bag, looking behind them. STRANGER
crosses TINBAD moving back to R; TINBAD moves
in behind him even more closely, right on his
heels. As they cross R ALI WHEY and BAK ALI
are startled to see TINBAD coming towards them.)

ALI WHEY   Plan A!

(He puts the loot bag behind his back with one hand
and claps the other to his face. BAK ALI also claps
a hand to his face. They take them away to reveal
ALI WHEY with a large false moustache and BAK
ALI with a very unconvincing set of joke teeth. The
STRANGER and TINBAD take no notice of them and
continue off R.)

BAK ALI   (speaking with difficulty) That fooled him. (realises
he is wearing the joke teeth and takes them out)

SINBAD THE SAILOR

Oh, sorry - this is plan B.

ALI WHEY   (removing his moustache) Never mind, it worked. Now we can divide the spoils.

BAK ALI   No, first let's share out the loot.

ALI WHEY   If you insist.

(He tips twelve large purses out of the bag in C and they kneel behind them, ALI WHEY L and BAK ALI R.)

Now, equal shares, of course.

BAK ALI   Of course. So you'd better leave it to me. I have a keen mathematical brain. To start with here's one for me and one for you. How's that for equality?

ALI WHEY   Spot on.

BAK ALI   Good. That brings us to two. I told you I had a keen mathematical brain. So here's one, two for me - (he counts in the one he already has and adds another) and one, two for you. (adds two purses to ALI WHEY's pile) Now one, two, three for me - (again counts in those he has and adds one) and one two, three for you. (adds three purses to ALI WHEY's pile) And - (looks at difference between the piles) wait a minute. Somehow you're getting more equal than I am.

ALI WHEY   So I am.

BAK ALI   I've got it. Let's change places.

(As they do MRS SINBAD and SINBAD enter R. They recognise and are about to accost ALI WHEY and BAK ALI but decide to wait and see what they are up to first.)

Right, I'll equal things up. We got to three, so here's one, two, three four for you - (takes four purses from L pile and puts them onto R) and one, two,three, four for me. (counts the two he has remaining and adds two) And one, two, three, four, five for you - (puts the remaining purse in C on to R pile and - without realising - transfers the four from the L pile to the R) And... Ali! It's all gone! (crawls L looking for it)

ALI WHEY   (crawling after him so that he is clear of purses)
                What? There must be a thief here .

                (MRS SINBAD and SINBAD move in behind the
                deserted purses.)

BAK ALI   I know that! There's two thieves here - us! We
                stole it from Mrs Sinbad.

                (MRS SINBAD and SINBAD exchange outraged looks
                and start stuffing the purses back into the loot bag.)

                But somebody else has been and scooped the pool.

SINBAD &   Us!
MRS SINBAD

ALI WHEY &   What? Aaaah!
BAK ALI

                (They jump up and start running L to the Chase
MUSIC 39   Music.)

SINBAD   After them!

                (MRS SINBAD and SINBAD start after them, but
                ALI WHEY and BAK ALI have met the wall and are
                running on the spot.)

ALI WHEY   Excuse me.

MRS SINBAD   Yes?

ALI WHEY   Do you mind if we run the other way?

MRS SINBAD   Be our guests.

ALI WHEY   Thank you.

                (ALI WHEY and BAK ALI run past them to R.)

SINBAD   Mother!

                (They follow ALI WHEY and BAK ALI off R, crossing
                the STRANGER - still being tailed by TINBAD -
                moving fairly fast R to L. Blocked again by the wall
                the STRANGER goes over the L steps into the Audi-
                torium and out by a nearby exit, TINBAD following.
                ALI WHEY and BAK ALI run in through an opposite
                Auditorium door and up R steps on to stage, to be
                foiled by the wall again. They run back to L, into
                the arms of SINBAD and MRS SINBAD who enter L
                on stage.)

SINBAD   Got you!

ALI WHEY &
BAK ALI   (going on to knees) Spare us!

SINBAD   Spare you? You kidnapped three people, sold my
                Princess into slavery –

MRS SINBAD   Pinched all our money –

SINBAD   And you ask us to spare you? Do you know the
                penalty just for theft in Cairo?

ALI WHEY   No!

BAK ALI   And we'd rather not find out.

SINBAD   Well, you're going to! First they hang, draw and
                quarter you –

ALI WHEY &
BAK ALI   Ooooooooh!

MRS SINBAD   Then they kill you – twice!

ALI WHEY &
BAK ALI   Aaaaaaah!

BAK ALI   That could be fatal.

SINBAD   But if you help us rescue Yasmin we might – just
                might – let you off.

ALI WHEY &
BAK ALI   Oh, we will! We will!

SINBAD   Then first of all, find out who bought the Princess
                and where she's being taken.

                (ALI WHEY and BAK ALI get up off knees.)

ALI WHEY   That might be tricky.

MUSIC 40   (Following Music The STRANGER and TINBAD come
                pelting back from where they went out in the audi-
                torium, over the L steps and start crossing in front
                of the others.)

BAK ALI   Leave it to me. Hey, you!

                (STRANGER double marks time, as does TINBAD.)

                Who are you?

                (STRANGER whispers in his ear.)

Oh... And where's that slave you bought being taken tc?

(STRANGER whispers to him again.)

Ah!

(STRANGER starts running again and exits R still followed by TINBAD.)

ALL THREE   What did he say?

BAK ALI   I don't know, I couldn't hear.

                (They are about to set on him when TINBAD runs on R.)

TINBAD   Well, I did! I bugged my umbrella. He's the Khedive of Egypt's Vizier and the Princess is being taken to the Khedive's desert camp!

SINBAD   Then we must go to the desert. (points to sign) Look - to the desert!

                (Enter DRUSILA R.)

ALL   To the desert!

                (They move L and meet wall.)

                Oh!

DRUSILA   (laughing - highly amused)

MRS SINBAD   Drusila! You're back!

BAK ALI   No, I'm Bak.

MRS SINBAD   I don't wish to know that. Drusila, I'm so pleased to see you again. And you're just in time to help us. You're a ship of the desert, dear, but where is the desert?

DRUSILA   (indicates R)

MRS SINBAD   (turning to sign) But it says there -

                (The sign snaps over to point R, still saying 'TO THE DESERT' and a concealed sign below it also snaps over - 'THE PRETTY WAY'.)

                Oh, how nice. Then -

ALL   To the desert!

SINBAD THE SAILOR

MUSIC 41   (OLD MAN Music Green spot onto the OLD MAN
                  OF THE SEA as he pokes his head over the wall L.
                  Start to fade lights and close traverse tabs. Fly
                  frontcloth.)

OLD MAN   The desert, yes! Oh, shut your traps!
                  Well, as a bit of fun, perhaps,
                  I'll go there too, but in disguise.
                  'Twill give them such a nice surprise!

MUSIC 42   (As the OLD MAN OF THE SEA disappears PERI
                  Music plays and white spot on to PERI as she
                  enters R.)

PERI   And now what mischief are you brewing?
                  To find out just what you are doing
                  I'll hie me to the desert too –
                  'Twill be a nice surprise for you!

                  (BLACKOUT
MUSIC 43   Eastern Music   Strike wall. Open traverse tabs.)

II - 3 - 74   SCENE 3   The KHEDIVE's Desert Camp

                  (Fullset. A desert scene. Cut-out ground row on
                  back of rostrum of a distant Pyramid or two and
                  lots of sand dunes. L is a clump of palm trees. R
                  a rich Arab-style tent. In front of its open entrance
                  is a pile of luxurious cushions.
                  Lights up – evening – the KHEDIVE OF EGYPT is
                  discovered reclining on the cushions smoking a
                  hookah, with his VIZIER – the STRANGER – and
                  ATTENDANTS around him   – CHORUS and CHILDREN
                  as ATTENDANTS – MUSIC 43 continues under his
                  opening speech.)

KHEDIVE   Night in the desert. Stars shining brightly in a
                  velvet sky. The clear desert air wafting on a gentle
                  breeze to blow away the heat of the day. The camels
                  have lain down their burdens, men rest from their
                  toil and all is very peaceful.

                  (ALL nod in sage agreement. MUSIC 43 ends.)

                  And very boring.

                  (ALL nod in even sager agreement.)

I can't spend the entire evening smoking this thing and every so often saying 'Ah, Condor.' Besides, it's bad for me. Well, it has been ever since they stuck a Government Health Warning on it. (points to label on Hookah bottle) But what else can I do?

(SINBAD looks cautiously on from behind palm trees.)

(suddenly bellowing) Well, tell me, somebody!

(SINBAD withdraws. Dismay and urgent whispered consultations between the ATTENDANTS, as a result of which the VIZIER bends down and whispers in the KHEDIVE's ear. KHEDIVE's face lights up.)

Splendid! Of course, my new slave.

(SINBAD looks on again.)

Fetch her!

(VIZIER claps his hands, which is passed on down a line of clapping hands.)

I said 'fetch her', not give her a round of applause.

(PAGE scurries into tent.)

And take this thing away.

(ATTENDANT removes Hookah. GUARD enters R from tent with YASMIN. SINBAD reacts.)

Ah, delightful. Well done, Vizier. Definitely this week's best buy. Turn round, my dear.

(Unwillingly YASMIN turns round.)

Good, good. I just wanted to make sure nobody had stuck any Government Health Warnings on you. Well, let's not waste time. Come to my arms!

(SINBAD can't restrain himself from stepping forward. YASMIN sees him.)

YASMIN   Sinbad!

(SINBAD motions caution and steps back.)

KHEDIVE   Well, yes, sin is bad. But it's also very nice. So, come to my arms!

(YASMIN doesn't move. GUARD pushes her. She flashes him an indignant look then perches rather primly on the edge of a cushion away from the KHEDIVE.)

Don't be afraid. I am but a man as other men.

YASMIN   I know. In fact, you remind me of another man.

KHEDIVE   And who is that, my petal?

YASMIN   My grandfather. Only he is much younger looking than you, of course.

KHEDIVE   (to VIZIER) Stupid idea of yours. Take her away!

(GUARD removes YASMIN into tent, somewhat roughly, to SINBAD's indignation.)

Have we no entertainers in camp? No camp followers?

(This gives SINBAD an idea and he disappears. Meanwhile the VIZIER is whispering to KHEDIVE.)

Oh, yes. I got rid of the last lot of camp followers, didn't I? They were a bit too camp. Pity though, I'd have liked a few dancers or something.

(SINBAD enters L motioning for the others to follow him on stage. VIZIER sees him and whispers to KHEDIVE.)

A stranger approaching? Ah, probably the delivery man from Harrods.

SINBAD   (salaams) O most mighty ruler, forgive such a lowly creature as I for chancing to overhear your wish, but it so happens I have with me the most famous troupe of dancers in all Egypt.

KHEDIVE   Excellent. Let them appear.

SINBAD   At once, Excellency. (aside to off L) Come on! (turns back and salaams again to KHEDIVE) The Dancing - er - Sintinalibaks!

(TINBAD enters L, salaams and squats down. He produces an Arab flute with a bulbous end - see 'Special Instructions' - He puts the wrong end to his mouth. - EFFECT 16 Opening bars of Beethoven's 5th -)

TINBAD   Sorry, wrong side.

(He reverses the flute and starts to blow. - EFFECT
17 Few pathetic wails - The flute starts to bend in
the middle and the wails get more distorted ending
with a raspberry. TINBAD hastily puts flute down.)

That was the overture.

KHEDIVE   Well, I'm glad it's over anyway.

(TINBAD produces a small hand drum and starts
to play it. MRS SINBAD in yashmak and Eastern
trousers etc enters L with ALI WHEY and BAK ALI
in long close-fitting Egyptian robes and tarbooshes
following.)

MUSIC 44   The Dancing School in Cairo

MRS SINBAD,   Dancers extraordinary,
ALI WHEY &   We can set your blood on fire-o;
BAK ALI   We have come to entertain you
                    From the Dancing School in Cairo.
                We all went to ballet classes -
                    Not a single one's a tyro -
                'Les Sylphides' through to 'Petroushka'
                    In the Dancing School in Cairo.

ALI WHEY   Watch our assembles and jetes;

BAK ALI   See our thirty-two fouettes.

MRS SINBAD   We have danced in ev'ry disco,
                Camden Town to San Francisco.

TINBAD   You can either give a cheque
                    Or you can pay Post Office Giro -

ALL FOUR   We'll take anybody's money
                    In the Dancing School in Cairo.

                We are dancers most spectacular,
                    Available on hire-o

MRS SINBAD   Ring three times and ask for Lulu

ALL FOUR   At the Dancing School in Cairo.

TINBAD   If you went to dancing classes
                    In a town in Hertfordshire-o
                You would find them rather tame
                    Beside the Dancing School in Cairo.

BAK ALI   Watch our lifts and elevations;

ALI WHEY   Hold your breath at our gyrations;

MRS SINBAD   Artistry in ev'ry posture –
               If you want us it will cost yer.

ALL FOUR   Since we're running out of rhymes,
                   Will you please write us some in Biro.
               You will win the gratitude
                   Of all the Dancing School –
                   The Dancing School in Cairo!

KHEDIVE   Hmm, well certainly unusual. Still, some
               refreshments for the dancers.

BAK ALI   Oh yes, I could just go a pint.

MRS SINBAD   I'll have a small port and lemon. No, come to
               think of it, a small lemon and port.

               (SINBAD,during the dance, has entered the tent in
               search of YASMIN, and they now emerge and are
               about to make off into the desert when the KHEDIVE
               sees them.)

KHEDIVE   What's this? My new slave, just wandering about.
               What is the meaning of this?

               (SINBAD and YASMIN stop and exchange worried
               looks.)

MRS SINBAD   (aside to ALI WHEY and BAK ALI) This looks
               dicey. Get Drusila.

               (ALI WHEY and BAK ALI slip off R, unobserved.)

KHEDIVE   Answer me! What is the meaning of this?

YASMIN   You are! I couldn't resist you any more. You're
               so handsome! So manly! So virile! So –

SINBAD   (aside) Don't overdo it!

KHEDIVE   This is more like it. You were about to say, so –?

YASMIN   So – er – so I came out.

KHEDIVE   Naturally. Well, in that case –

               (OLD MAN OF THE SEA enters L disguised as a
               Turkish carpet seller, carrying three carpets,
               which he puts on ground.)

OLD MAN	Carpets for sale! Fine Turkish carpets!
KHEDIVE	Carpets! Don't bother me with carpets just when things are looking up.
OLD MAN	But these are very special carpets. Perhaps the young lady would like to step on this one and feel the softness, the quality, the -
YASMIN	No, I don't think I would.
KHEDIVE	You might as well. He'll be on about them all night otherwise, and I have - other plans.
	(YASMIN reluctantly steps on carpet. OLD MAN OF THE SEA immediately throws off his disguise and jumps on carpet too.)
OLD MAN	Aha!
	(He makes a magic pass. Flash - BLACKOUT - lights up. YASMIN, OLD MAN OF THE SEA and the carpet have disappeared. There is general consternation.)
SINBAD	Yasmin! That must have been -
	(OLD MAN OF THE SEA's laughter is heard off. White flash R and PERI appears.)
PERI	You've guessed, The Old Man of the Sea, the pest! To India now he's on his way, But that's a game that two can play - Stand there! (indicates carpet to SINBAD) And both of you, stand there! (indicates to MRS SINBAD and TINBAD to stand on 3rd **carpet**) Now you can chase him through the air!
MUSIC 45	(She makes a magic pass. Flash - BLACKOUT - lights up. PERI, SINBAD, MRS SINBAD, TINBAD and the two remaining carpets have disappeared. There is more consternation. DRUSILA, ALI WHEY and BAK ALI run on. Flying Carpet Music Cut-outs of two figures on a carpet, followed by one figure on a carpet, followed by two figures on a carpet go across the sky L to R.)
ALI WHEY	Hey, come back! What about us?
KHEDIVE	You? Seize them!

MUSIC 46

(Strobe Music ALI WHEY, BAK ALI and DRUSILA run to L and VIZIER leads ATTENDANTS in chase after them. BLACKOUT - up strobe light. Close traverse tabs. For a while the chasers and the chased maintain their distance. But the pursued put on a spurt and manage to increase the lead. ALI WHEY puts up his hand and ALL stop. Up stage lights, cut strobe. ALL have a hearty pant. ALI WHEY nods - BLACKOUT - up strobe light. ALL start running again. DRUSILA, ALI WHEY and BAK ALI run off L. VIZIER and ATTENDANTS move towards L exit. ALI WHEY appears R running behind them. He realizes and stops and waves to the figures who are disappearing off L. BAK ALI runs on R.)

BAK ALI   Hey! We're behind you!

ALI WHEY   Shut up!

(They turn tail and run off R. The pursuers turn and run L to R after them.
BLACKOUT   Open traverse tabs.)

II - 4 - 80   SCENE 4   In the Air and on the Ground

(Gauze cloth if possible in front of rostrum. Ground row, about 2' 6" high on front of rostrum. Dry ice swirls in front of ground row. Cloud wings L and R. A cloud machine sends clouds racing across the cyclorama from R to L. The lights come up

MUSIC 47

behind gauze and we see the **OLD** MAN OF THE SEA and YASMIN apparently seated on their carpet in C. - see 'Special Instructions' - YASMIN is distressed, the OLD MAN OF THE SEA exultant, until he looks behind him to L. Immediately he urges his carpet to go faster. He and YASMIN move to RC as SINBAD enters L with a similar carpet frame. He moves to C and is followed by MRS SINBAD and TINBAD, also with carpet frame, who come to LC.

OLD MAN OF THE SEA and YASMIN hit an air pocket and dip accordingly. Then SINBAD meets it, followed by MRS SINBAD and TINBAD.

SINBAD moves towards OLD MAN OF **THE SEA** and YASMIN, who drop back a little at the same time.

OLD MAN OF THE SEA makes his carpet swoop forward and makes a magic pass at SINBAD. SINBAD begins to drop back to L.

MRS SINEAD and TINBAD exchange a look, then TINBAD whips up their carpet with his umbrella - like a jockey. They overtake SINBAD moving to C whilst he drops back to LC. TINBAD gets carried away and they now overtake the OLD MAN OF THE SEA and YASMIN moving RC whilst the OLD MAN OF THE SEA and YASMIN drop back to C.

Realising that they have been too successful MRS SINBAD puts on a policewoman's cap and TINBAD a policeman's helmet. He then opens and holds up his umbrella with a flashing blue light on the top of it. - EFFECT 18 Police siren - They wave the OLD MAN OF THE SEA down and start to drop back towards him.

OLD MAN OF THE SEA makes his carpet give a sudden spurt forward. He bumps MRS SINBAD's and TINBAD's carpet, then gets the front of his carpet under the back of theirs to tip them up and they disappear off R with cries of distress.

Music changes to falling motif as the OLD MAN OF THE SEA delighted and YASMIN distressed again,exit R. SINBAD moves to R looking in a worried way downwards and behind him and the lights fade to BLACKOUT.

- EFFECT 19 Loud bump off L - and a cry of pain from TINBAD. A little more falling music and - EFFECT 20 2nd Loud bump off L - and a cry from MRS SINBAD. A frontcloth of a rocky mountain pass has been let in during this and now the lights come up on it. MRS SINBAD rolls on from L and lands flat on her face.)

MRS SINBAD   Well! I think that was a close encounter of the third kind. (rises and adjusts bosom) Ooh! Also the first and second kind; and it wasn't at all kind! And now I ve lost everybody. Mr Tinbad can't be far away, but I wonder where Drusila and those other two are? I wouldn't like to lose Drusila, you know, because I'm really very fond of her. In fact,

I wrote a little song about her. Would you like to
hear it? (audience reation) That's good, because
you were going to anyway.

MUSIC 48   Dromedary   (Words for Song Sheet)

> You may cheer the hero -
> Hurray! Hurray! Hurray!
> You may hiss the villain -
> Yah! Hiss! Boo!
> You may find the baddies rather scary;
> But all say 'Pleased to meet yer' -
> Very pleased to meet yer!
> To that amazing creature -
> What amazing creature?
> The very wary, hairy Dromedary.

Now, if only they could all hear that they might
find their way here. But my voice isn't loud enough on its own, I need some help. Can you sing?
(audience reaction) Then I'm going to take an
unprecedented step. I'm going to ask you to sing
my song! That surprised you, eh? (audience reaction) No?

(Song sheet starts to drop in behind her.)

Well, I assure you it was just a little thought on
the spur of the moment. (sees song sheet, to
off stage) You sillies, you've given the game
away. (to audience) Anyway, I'm sure it'll help
them all to find their way here, so sing as loud as
you can. And -

(Audience starts singing. MRS SINBAD looks very
disappointed and lets them trail away.)

No, no, no, we want them to get here today not
next week. Now then, really let yourselves go.
And -

(Audience sings.)

Well, somebody might have heard that.

(TINBAD bursts in at rear of Auditorium.)

TINBAD   I did!

MRS SINBAD   Mr Tinbad!

(DRUSILA, ALI WHEY and BAK ALI run on L.)

ALI WHEY & BAK ALI	So did we!
ALI WHEY	All the way from the Khedive's camp.
BAK ALI	Lovely quality, too, brought a tear to my eye.
TINBAD	Yes indeed, all those childish trebles. In fact, I'm going to suggest something astounding.
OTHER THREE	Yes?
TINBAD	Let's get some of the children up here to sing it.
OTHER THREE	Revolutionary!

(Ad lib whilst getting children up on to stage to sing song, and also whilst getting them back to their places.)

MRS SINBAD   (when everyone is seated again) Right, one last time and really lift the roof off.

(As audience sing for last time fly out song sheet, close traverse tabs and fly out frontcloth. ALL exit at end of number.
BLACKOUT Open traverse tabs.)

SCENE 5 An Indian Jungle Clearing   II - 5 - 83

MUSIC 49

(Fullset. A lush jungle setting. There is a high groundrow covering the front of the rostrum. Tree wing R. A curtain of tangled creepers L. A little onstage of it is a large creeper covered rock, which has a fragment of material on it. There is an old log C. MONKEY Dance Lights up and the CHILDREN as MONKEYS are discovered. They exit at end of their dance. YASMIN enters L through the creeper curtain, dress slightly torn.)

YASMIN   Oh, blow my silly father! It's all his fault, wanting to send me to India to get married. I'd live in such luxury, he said. Well, here I am in India and just look at the luxury - that palatial pile of tangled old creepers, with a floor of the very finest mud to sleep on. Well done, father! And yet, if it hadn't been for him, I wouldn't have met Sinbad. But that's

the hardest thing of all. Now that I have met him
it's so unbearable to be without him.

MUSIC 50   Without Him

Without him there would be no more sun
    And the world would be dark without him.
Without him all the blossoms would die
    And my heart would not beat without him.
There would be no more tomorrows;
    Fires would flicker out and die.
Only left would be the sorrows,
    Ev'ry breath would be a sigh.
I can't do without him. Not a song-bird would sing,
Not without him. There would be no more Spring,
    Not without him, without him, without him.

Find a road without a bend,
A treasure at the rainbow's end;
Try to find the crock of gold,
Alone and lonely, growing old.

There would be no more tomorrows, etc

(OLD MAN OF THE SEA enters through creepers L.)

Ugh! You! How horrid!

OLD MAN   Thanks a lot.
They love me though. (audience reaction)
                              Well, maybe not.
Ah well, despite your unkind greeting
I've plann'd for you a special meeting.

YASMIN   Who with?

OLD MAN   Why, him for whom you sigh,
I thought you'd like to see him - die!

YASMIN   Oh, no!

OLD MAN   Oh, yes! But not too soon;
So there's no need to mope or moon.
That love needs time I understand,
And so a long slow death I've plann'd.

YASMIN   You beast! You fiend! You -

OLD MAN   Careful, please!
No naughty words, you'll shock the trees.

Besides young Sinbad might be near,
I left some clues to draw him here. (listens)
Ah, yes, I think -

YASMIN   Sinbad, look out!

OLD MAN   I'll pay you for that wanton shout! (drags her L)
In there!

YASMIN   I won't!   (stamps on his gouty foot)

OLD MAN   Ow, help! That hurt!

YASMIN   I'm glad!

OLD MAN   Then you with danger flirt.
Get in!   (he half pushes her through creepers)

YASMIN   I'll scream!

OLD MAN   One peep or cry
And on the instant you'll both die! (thrusts her
through and out of sight)
And now a small disguise I need.
And I mean very small indeed!

(He moves behind the rock piece and crouches
down slowly, finally disappearing behind rock as
if he's shrinking. A moment later a smaller ver-
sion of him appears - CHILD double - from behind
the rock. The LITTLE OLD MAN sniggers.)

LITTLE OLD MAN   Ah, just in time!

(He sits in front of the rock looking very feeble and
pretending to be asleep. SINBAD enters R, with his
jacket slung over his shoulder and a small piece or
two of material in his hand.)

SINBAD   Whew! It's hot work tracking in the jungle; and I
hope I'm still on the right track. I found these bits
of Yasmin's dress back there, but I haven't seen
any - wait a minute, is that - ? (crosses and takes
piece of material from rock) It is! Then I'm right!

(LITTLE OLD MAN stirs.)

I'm sorry. I didn't mean to wake you. I wonder,
though, have you seen a beautiful young girl and a
horrible old man come this way?

(LITTLE OLD MAN nods feebly.)

SINBAD THE SAILOR

You have! Do you know where they've gone?

LITTLE OLD MAN   Yes, but I'm too old and weak to show you. But if you could carry me -

SINBAD   Of course! Here, climb on my shoulders.

(He kneels and puts his jacket down. Delighted, the LITTLE OLD MAN climbs on his shoulders and SINBAD stands - if it is impossible for the actress playing SINBAD to rise from kneeling with a child on her shoulders, have the LITTLE OLD MAN sit on the rock piece and climb on to SINBAD from there.)

All right?

LITTLE OLD MAN   Yes! Now you never will be free
From me, the Old Man of the Sea!

(SINBAD struggles to get him off. LITTLE OLD MAN squeezes his neck with his knees.)

SINBAD   You're choking me!

LITTLE OLD MAN   I know, my friend,
And that is how you'll meet your end,
When I declare your time has come.
Yasmin!

(YASMIN runs on L through creeper curtain.)

YASMIN   Sinbad!

LITTLE OLD MAN   Yes, here's your chum!
But now's no time for idle talk,
The sun grows high, let's take a walk
Within the jungle's shady trees.
So, gee up!

SINBAD   No!

LITTLE OLD MAN   I'll use my knees!

(He does so and SINBAD starts to move forward.)

YASMIN   You swine!

LITTLE OLD MAN   I love to hear you yelp,
Especially when there's none to help.
(kicks SINBAD's ribs like a jockey)
Come on!

(SINBAD staggers off L with LITTLE OLD MAN.)

YASMIN
He's right, there is no one.

MUSIC 51
(White flash R and PERI appears holding the bottle in which SINBAD found her.)

PERI
There's me. He can't have all the fun.
To foil the wretch, though, we must hurry.

YASMIN
But who - ?

PERI
I'm on your side, don't worry.
But you must do just as I say.
When they return ask if you may
Give Sinbad this. (gives YASMIN the bottle)

YASMIN
What's in it?

PERI
Wine,
Mix'd in a special way of mine
With certain herbs. It needs as yet
One more. That only you can get.

YASMIN
What herb is that?

PERI
It's dragon's eye.

YASMIN
I know it. Only me, though - why?

PERI
Pluck'd by a maiden's hand at noon
It gives the draught a final boon
And turns it to a magic brew.

YASMIN
But -

PERI
Trust me. You'll find if you do
All will come right. The sun's rays tell
It's nigh on noon. Be swift! Farewell! (exit R)

YASMIN
Well, I don't know who she was, but somehow I feel I can trust her. I hope so because I can't think of any other way to help Sinbad. Anyway, here goes.

(Exit YASMIN L. MRS SINBAD enters R, followed by TINBAD, ALI WHEY and BAK ALI. TINBAD is looking at a guide book.)

MRS SINBAD
No sign of Sinbad yet. Yes, there is - his jacket, look!

(They stop and MRS SINBAD bends to pick it up

just as DRUSILA gallops on behind them. She has the loot bag attached to her hump. She bumps in to BAK ALI, who bumps into ALI WHEY, who bumps into TINBAD, who bumps into MRS SINBAD and knocks her over. DRUSILA is amused.)

ALL   Drusila!

MRS SINBAD   Silly girl. Anyway, Sinbad must be somewhere near. We'll just have to look around for him. I wonder where we are, though.

BAK ALI   Ah, I can tell you that.

MRS SINBAD   Oh, good. Where are we then?

BAK ALI   Here.

MRS SINBAD   Er - yes. Very helpful.

BAK ALI   Don't mention it. I have an infallible bump of locality.

ALI WHEY   You'll have another one if you go on like that.

MRS SINBAD   Anything in the guide book we should look out for as we go along, Mr Tinbad?

TINBAD   Yes, it says here - 'note the colourful Boo-Boo bird'.

                 (A colourful bird shoots on and off L like a cuckoo in a clock.)

MRS SINBAD   I saw one! Why is it called a Boo-Boo?

TINBAD   It's related to the cuckoo.

BIRD   (shooting on and off twice) Boo-boo! Boo-boo!

TINBAD   It says - 'It also has the ability to imitate other birds' -

BIRD   (appearing) Tweet-tweet.

TINBAD   (still reading) 'but not very well'.

BIRD   What did you expect? Percy Edwards? (disappears)

TINBAD   'Boo-Boos often fly in flocks when they all make a'-

                 (- EFFECT 21 Several birds overhead calling 'Boo-boo'-   ALL clap a hand to their heads. DRUSILA laughs heartily until a straggler flies across,

- EFFECT 22 'Boo-boo'- and something obviously
thuds on DRUSILA's head. She stalks off R, highly
chagrined.)

MRS SINBAD   Oh dear, she'll sulk for hours now. Anyway, any-
                    thing else to look out for?

TINBAD   Yes, 'the lesser spotted Centipede'.

MRS SINBAD   Ooh, I don't like little creepy-crawlies.

ALI WHEY   Nor me.

BAK ALI   Nor me.

TINBAD   Ah, these won't worry you then, they grow to
                    about ten feet.

MRS SINBAD,
ALI WHEY &   Oh good. Ten feet!
BAK AL

TINBAD   But they're very rare.

MRS SINBAD   Just as well. I'd much rather find Sinbad than one
                    of those. Come on. (leads everyone off DL)

MUSIC 52   (CENTIPEDE Music A LESSER SPOTTED CENTIPEDE
                    (5 CHILDREN) enters DR and undulates across the
                    stage to exit DL. MRS SINBAD, TINBAD, ALI WHEY
                    and BAK ALI enter UL.)

                    Still no sign of Sinbad.

BAK ALI   Or the lesser spotted whatsit, thank goodness.

                    (CENTIPEDE follows on after him and continues in
                    line behind them as they exit UR. They enter DR
                    without CENTIPEDE.)

MRS SINBAD   Oh, it's too hot to go wandering about any more.
                    Sinbad's bound to come back for his jacket. Let's
                    just sit down and wait for him.

                    (They sit on the log, L to R MRS SINBAD, TINBAD,
                    ALI WHEY and BAK ALI.)

                    We can sing a little song while we're waiting.

                    (They sing, unaccompanied, some song such as
                    'One Finger, One Thumb Keep Moving'. CENTIPEDE
                    enters UR behind them. It nudges BAK ALI gently
                    with its head. He turns, sees it, tries to scream,

SINBAD THE SAILOR

	can't manage it and runs off R. The others continue singing. CENTIPEDE nudges ALI WHEY.)
ALI WHEY	Stop it, Bak, I'm singing.
	(CENTIPEDE nudges him again.)
	(turning) Oh, do be - WAAH!
	(He runs off L in front of the other two, CENTIPEDE exits L behind them.)
MRS SINBAD	What's the matter with him?
TINBAD	I don't know, but Bak's gone, too. So perhaps I can tell you that - (gulps and looks away) that whenever I'm with you - I - er - I -
MRS SINBAD	Yes?
TINBAD	I look at your face and - er -
MRS SINBAD	Yes, yes?
	(CENTIPEDE enters UL.)
TINBAD	And I want to say (turns back to her) - HELP! (bolts off R)
MRS SINBAD	Oh dear, and I thought we were getting on so well.
	(She moves down log, CENTIPEDE follows her.)
	Now I'm all alone. I don't feel alone, though. What was that? Did someone say I wasn't alone? (audience reaction) Who's here then? (audience reaction) A centipede? Not a lesser spotted one? (audience reaction) Well, where is it? (audience reaction) Behind me! I'll have a look. I'll do it very slowly and take it by surprise.
	(She turns anti-clockwise slowly, the CENTIPEDE following, the legs moving faster the nearer they are to the back.)
	(over shoulder) There's nothing here.
	(Audience reaction. She turns back and comes face to face with the CENTIPEDE. CENTIPEDE gives a cry and runs off R.)
	What? How dare you insult me, you rotten centipede!

(She runs off after it, bashing it with TINBAD's umbrella. YASMIN enters L with a small plant.)

YASMIN   Here it is, the dragon's eye plant.

LTTLE OLD MAN   (off) Come on!

YASMIN   Just in time. I'll get it ready.

(She exits L through creeper curtain. On rostrum behind the groundrow, we see the LITTLE OLD MAN being carried by SINBAD - R to L.)

LITTLE OLD MAN Faster, faster! And faster still!

SINBAD   I cannot.

LITTLE OLD MAN   You both can and will!

(They disappear L. YASMIN enters through the creeper curtain.)

YASMIN   This had better work. (sniffs it) Um, smells delicious.

(SINBAD staggers on L with LITTLE OLD MAN and collapses.)

LITTLE OLD MAN Get up! Come on, get off your knees!
                Get up, I say, or I shall-

YASMIN   Please!
                Let him refresh himself with this.

LITTLE OLD MAN Well, what a tender little miss!
                What is it?

YASMIN   Wine.

LITTLE OLD MAN   Then give it me! (he grabs the bottle greedily and drains it, finishing with a loud hiccough.)
                Oh, 'shlovely! Makesh me feel all free.

SINBAD   Then I'll be too! (throws LITTLE OLD MAN off)

LITTLE OLD MAN   Ah, help! I'm sinking!
                And worse than that, I think I'm shrinking!

MUSIC 53   (BLACKOUT Shrinking Music.)

                Aaaaaaaah!
                I'm going - going - gone! I've shrunk!

(Flash. Lights up on PERI holding a doll replica of LITTLE OLD MAN and the bottle she was originally imprisoned in.)

PERI   And just the size in here to dunk!

(LITTLE OLD MAN's cries are abruptly cut off when PERI puts the stopper in the bottle.)

There! That's put paid to him forever!
Now joy can crown all your endeavour.

(Exit PERI R.)

SINBAD   I think it has already - unless you don't want to marry me.

YASMIN   Try and stop me.

SINBAD   What about your father?

YASMIN   He couldn't stop me.

SINBAD   And King Serendib?

YASMIN   King Serendib? Who's he?

KING SERENDIB   (running on R) Me! (he is panting a bit as he looks to be very old) Quickly, hide me!

SINBAD   Why, what's the matter?

KING SERENDIB   Wives! And the Caliph of Baghdad! He's threatening me with another one if he can find her. But I've got two hundred already and look what it's done to me. I'm only thirty-five.

WIVES   (off R) Husband!

KING SERENDIB   Hide me!

YASMIN   In there!

(She bundles him through creeper curtain, the WIVES run on R, giggling.)

WIVES   Husband!

SINBAD   (pointing UL) That way!

(With more giggles they run off UL. MRS SINBAD and TINBAD enter DL.)

MRS SINBAD &   Sinbad!
TINBAD

SINBAD	Mother! Congratulate me. I'm getting married.
MRS SINBAD	(affected) Oh, my boy!
TINBAD	Congratulations!
	(The WIVES stream on UL screaming and run off UR. BAK ALI and ALI WHEY run on after them.)
BAK ALI	I tell you it's our powerful personalities.
ALI WHEY	Are you sure it's us?
BAK ALI	Yes. (sees something off L) NO!
	(He pelts off R. ALI WHEY turns and looks and, with a cry, scurries after him. CENTIPEDE chases across from L to R.)
CALIPH	(off R) King Serendib! (entering) Where is the fellow! (seeing her) Yasmin!
YASMIN	Father!
CALIPH	Come to my arms! Thank goodness I've found you. But now I've lost the silly fellow who's going to marry you.
YASMIN	You haven't, Father. He's here. Sinbad.
CALIPH	Sinbad? Nonsense! He's too poor. I couldn't think of -
MRS SINBAD	Poor? He's got twelve million sequins.
CALIPH	Of anyone more suitable. Where's the twelve million?
MRS SINBAD	Running around on four legs at the moment.
	(DRUSILA runs on L and bumps into MRS SINBAD.)
	Drusila! Still, you're just in time. Here it is.
CALIPH	Sinbad, take her, she's yours.
KING SERENDIB	(emerging) What a relief!
CALIPH	You shall be wed as soon as we get back - to Baghdad.
ALL	To Baghdad!
MUSIC 54	Baghdad (Reprise MUSIC 13)

SINBAD THE SAILOR

(Close traverse tabs during number.)

Baghdad, Baghdad!
    We've been long a-gone, Mum;
    Put the kettle on, Mum.
Pack your bag, Dad!
    We go with elation
    To the station.
Though we've had such fun abroad
    And going home is rather sad,
It has been a tiring journey
    All the way from old Baghdad.

(ALL exit except MRS SINBAD and TINBAD.)

SCENE 6   The Road to the Aisle

(Traverse tabs. Carry straight on from previous scene.)

TINBAD	Mrs Sinbad.
MRS SINBAD	Yes, Mr Tinbad?
TINBAD	We're all alone.
MRS SINBAD	So we are.
TINBAD	Mrs Sinbad ....
MRS SINBAD	Yes, Mr Tinbad?
TINBAD	You don't mind it I call you 'Mrs Sinbad'?
MRS SINBAD	Not at all.
TINBAD	You wouldn't like me to call you something else?
MRS SINBAD	No, I wouldn't know who you were talking to, Mr Tinbad.
TINBAD	No. But - well - I'll put it another way. You don't have to call me Mr Tinbad.
MRS SINBAD	Oh, very well. Tinbad, then.
TINBAD	I meant, I have another name.
MRS SINBAD	Tinbad, have you been leading a double life all this time?
TINBAD	No, no. A first name. Mustapha.

MRS SINBAD	What a coincidence! Mr Sinbad was a Mustapha too.
TINBAD	Oh, good. It'll be easy for you then.
MRS SINBAD	What will?
TINBAD	Mustapha.
MRS SINBAD	My name's not Mustapha.
TINBAD	No, I know, but what is - what is -
MRS SINBAD	Yes?
TINBAD	(gulps) What is -
MRS SINBAD	Yes, yes?
TINBAD	(mouthes soundlessly then aside to audience) I can't say it. Could you help me to say, 'What is your name?' (audience reaction) Oh, thank you. Then altogether - What is your name?
MRS SINBAD	Mrs Sinbad.
TINBAD	No, no, no, no, no, no, no, no, no, NO! Your first name.
MRS SINBAD	Well, why didn't you say so? It's - er - er - I had it on the tip of my tongue - er - I haven't used it for ages. Ah, of course! I remember, it's Fatima.
TINBAD	Fatima! How beautiful!
MRS SINBAD	Yes, it is nice, isn't it - Mustapha.
TINBAD	My friends call me Musty, Fatima.
MRS SINBAD	Do they? Well, my friends don't call me Fatty. Not if they want to stay my friends.
TINBAD	Oh, I do, I do! In fact I want to be more than a friend, because - (turns away and mumbles) I love you.
MRS SINBAD	I beg your pardon?
TINBAD	(a little louder) I love you.
MRS SINBAD	I still didn't catch.
	(DRUSILA enters beside TINBAD, just as he lifts his head and inadvertently bellows at her.)

TINBAD	I LOVE YOU!
DRUSILA	(looks at him in great surprise, then bursts into laughter and runs off)
TINBAD	Not her, Fatima - you. Will you at last be my little - little Fatima?
MRS SINBAD	Oh, Mustapha, this is so sudden. You must give me time to think. I've thought. Yes!
TINBAD	Yes?
MRS SINBAD	Yes - because I've already booked our wedding for this afternoon.
TINBAD	You have? Oh, you're so clever, Fatima.
MRS SINBAD	I am? Well, you're not so dusty - Musty.
MUSIC 55	Don't You?

TINBAD	Oh, oh, oh, I think you're simply wonderful,
	     Yes, I do, I do, I do.
	 I think you're great, first-rate, I do -
	     Don't you?

MRS SINBAD	Oh, oh, oh, I think you're simply marvellous,
	     Yes I do, I do, I do.
	 I think you're fine, divine, I do -
	     Don't you?

TINBAD	When you look in the mirror
MRS SINBAD	Up on the shelf,
TINBAD	Don't you feel funny?
MRS SINBAD	Leave yourself money?
BOTH	Aren't you crazy about yourself? Oh, oh, oh, I think you're simply glorious, Yes, I do, I do, I do.
MRS SINBAD	I think you're swell -
TINBAD	Like hell I do!
BOTH	Don't you? (dance) When you wake in the morning, Happy and bright,

Haven't you the theory
You are not the dreary
   Sort of person you were last night?

Oh, oh, oh, I think you're simply glorious,
   Yes, I do, I do, I do.

TINBAD   I think you're swell –

MRS SINBAD   Like hell I do!

BOTH   Don't you?

(As they exit open traverse tabs.)

SCENE 7 Palace of the Caliph of Baghdad   II - 7 - 97

(Fullset. Grand Eastern Palace scene with steps
down from rostrum in C.

MUSIC 56   Walk Down CHORUS and CHILDREN take their
bows and back away to form diagonal lines L and
R. Principals, after entering on rostrum and
coming down C to take their bows, back away and
form diagonal lines in front of CHORUS. PERI
from R and OLD MAN OF THE SEA from L backing
R and L; CALIPH from L backing L; DRUSILA from
R backing R; ALI WHEY and BAK ALI enter L and R
but both back L; TINBAD from L backing R; MRS
SINBAD from R backing R. Fanfare. ALL turn in
as YASMIN enters from L and SINBAD from R to
meet in C of rostrum.)

ALL   Hurray!

(SINBAD and YASMIN move down and Principals
come into line with them. CHORUS and CHILDREN
move on to steps and rostrum.)

SINBAD   Adventure I both sought and found,
And travelled half the world around.
But with adventure I've now done.

YASMIN   Oh, no! Your best one's just begun.

OLD MAN   To say farewell I'm out the bottle.

PERI   Why, don't you like it?

OLD MAN   Not a lottle.

SINBAD THE SAILOR

(Others groan. DRUSILA kills herself laughing.)

MRS SINBAD   I think Drusila's getting dafter,
But she'll laugh happy ever after.
Me too, now that I've changed to Tin.

TINBAD   Ah well, of course, you gave up Sin.

SINBAD   Let's say goodnight before our rhymes get frailer.

ALL   Goodnight!

SINBAD   From them and me, Sinbad the Sailor!

MUSIC 57   Grand Finale   (reprise Music 13)

ALL   Show is over.
    Thank you very much for your participating.
That's it! Goodbye!
    Right outside the door your bus is waiting.
It has been most satisfactory -
    Bad was wrong and good was right.
Now we've run clean out of story,
    So God bless you and Goodnight.

        CURTAIN

www.ingramcontent.com/pod-product-compliance
Lightning Source LLC
LaVergne TN
LVHW051746080426
835511LV00018B/3248